APPARENTLY I'M NOT
EVERYONE'S CUP OF TEA

APPARENTLY i'M NOT EVERYONE'S CUP OF TEA

Graham Phipps

DISCLAIMER

In order to protect service user / client confidentiality, several details,
including names, ages and even gender have been changed where appropriate. Some
characters are an amalgam of two or three people. However apart from a small sprinkling
of artistic license, the life situations, dilemmas and childhood memories are all too real. My
imagination is not extensive enough to have made them up.

Matador
Unit E2 Airfield Business Park,
Harrison Road, Market Harborough,
Leicestershire. LE16 7UL
Tel: 0116 279 2299
Email: books@troubador.co.uk
Web: www.troubador.co.uk/matador
Twitter: @matadorbooks

ISBN 978 1803130 538

British Library Cataloguing in Publication Data.
A catalogue record for this book is available from the British Library.

Printed and bound in Great Britain by 4edge Limited
Typeset in 11pt Minion Pro by Troubador Publishing Ltd, Leicester, UK

Matador is an imprint of Troubador Publishing Ltd

To Shirl my long suffering wife, my four grown up children and my gorgeous grandchildren, all of whom struggle to keep me in the twenty first century.

Apparently I'm Not Everyone's Cup of Tea gives an often humorous insight into working with various groups of people who, on the face of it, needed some support but often chose to ignore me. The title comes from a remark given to me by a lady client who then disappeared into the toilet with book in hand.

ONE

A NEW JOB

I was asked to accompany a lady I supported to her doctor's appointment. I had assumed it was to do with her mental health issues, but was surprised to hear the lady doctor after taking a puzzled glance at me, turn to my client and ask, "Are you sure you want your support worker to be in the room with you?"

"Yes that's okay," came the reply.

I came out of the surgery twenty minutes later a lot wiser as regards the workings of the private parts of the female anatomy. I obviously hadn't learnt the, "Be prepared for the unexpected" lesson, I would have to do better in future.

It all started in January 2003, and with a heavy heart I knocked on the door of a 1970s semi-detached house in a quiet street. After what seemed an age, the door was opened by a lady in her forties. She smiled as she bent her head towards the room that I gathered the interview was to take place in. She ushered me in, seemed to change her mind as to where I should be seated, then pointed to a chair in an adjacent room. Sitting down I tried to make myself as comfortable as I could. She disappeared for a minute, then returned.

"Would you like a cup of tea?" she asked. I replied in the affirmative, sounding keener than I felt. My experience with cups of tea in strangers' houses was not good, and I always anticipated that off-putting stain that seemed to appear, usually after I had taken a few sips. She disappeared again but returned within seconds.

"Green milk or red?"

"Oh red please." Once more she disappeared only to return with another question.

"Sugar?"

"Yes one lump please." The next time she returned she brought with her a tray, pulled up a small table, and placed it next to my chair before she left the room. I waited and waited but I never did get to see that cup of tea. I realised there and then that working with people who needed some support in a residential setting was never going to be straightforward.

I had volunteered for redundancy at a local engineering works the month before, which was immediately, it seemed, granted. I thought the management might at least put in a protest but they didn't, and I found myself with mixed emotions looking for employment. Here I was, applying for a job at a well-known charity, working with vulnerable people. In the 1970s before machines became automated I made my industrial working life easier and more fulfilling by creating bespoke computer programmes, albeit written in Basic. Going to work was almost, but not quite, a pleasure. However as the decades rolled by automation, and off-the-shelf programmes became the norm, pressing a button or two to enable a machine to punch multiple components from a sheet of metal was not my idea of mental stimulation. Quite simply enough was enough and I needed to find another avenue of opportunity, in short a different way of working altogether.

I can't recall the interview going particularly well as I tried to remember certain pre-prepared facts and anecdotes, but the manager and her deputy must have taken pity on me, as with no qualifications with this type of work I was offered fifteen hours a week. This was a start but I realised I would have to find another part-time job if I was going to maintain a reasonable standard of living and put food on the table for my wife, four children, and to a much lesser extent numerous savage rodents that the kids called pets. I had given up making it big on the rock scene as the band Ultrasonic Intestine, a heady mix of punk, rock and female interference ("how much longer do you need to keep practising?") had long since given up. Judging by our one and only gig, practice was an ingredient that we did need in abundance. Seldom had anyone seen the pub's toilets so full. The only people left on the dance floor were the people who couldn't be bothered to queue. Still, the then-girlfriends did us proud as they tried to make sense of questionable versions of once-popular songs. People remarked afterwards how clever they were in adapting their dance to cater for the quickly shifting rhythms, as we experimented with changes of keys, bum notes and half remembered lyrics. The fact that we didn't always finish together didn't go unnoticed either. People can be so cruel.

On the first day of my new job I was introduced to the six residents. They resided in two semis, three in each, with the office-cum-bedroom sandwiched between them. This was designed for easy access to both houses. After reading the dos and don'ts, and after taking in some of the health and safety policies, I was given my first solo task; cooking the dinner for house one. I stared long and hard at the day's menu; it was cheese and potato pie. My confused silence was brought to an end by Anna, one of the residents, who smiled enquiringly at me and said, "I wish I was clever enough to cook cheese and potato pie." I respected her opinion, as I too was wishing I was knowledgeable in that respect. I decided it might be quicker to seek out a recipe. After searching in vain, I resorted to asking the support worker in the other house. Things didn't get much better when the second task of the evening was revealed to me. It seemed I was expected to carry out the ironing.

Comments such as "Molly doesn't do it like that, her shirts don't have any lumps in them and is it really necessary to iron handkerchiefs?" didn't help. In the end Anna took pity on me and declared that her blouses didn't really need ironing after all.

Despite a few initial mishaps during a steep learning curve I seemed to gel with the residents who proved to be a great bunch and often threw in the odd bit of helpful advice. I learnt at an early stage to ensure that there was enough cheese to go round. Tempers were frayed, fights were in danger of breaking out and more than one cup was smashed on the floor. Aside from this, meal times were relatively peaceful and to some extent food was shared evenly. In case I ever had occasion to drive them to a function I decided to sell my motorbike and purchase a car, as I doubted any of them would make good pillion passengers. It wasn't a hard decision in any case as I'd never really built up courage following an accident a few years back.

On a cold February morning I found myself lying spread-eagled across a mini roundabout.

"Don't move," shouted a concerned voice, but if there was something I'd learnt during those heart-stopping few moments it was that roads such as the one I was on were sodding dangerous, and taking stock of one's bits and pieces on one was not to be recommended. I hobbled across to safety and towards the driver of the car, the guilty party in this scenario. I suppose I'd already made a nodding sort of acquaintanceship with him, as I was sliding up the bonnet of his car. He was wearing a rather silly aghast expression and wondering if he would be in for a torrid time. His stance did little to help matters either, legs slightly bent, trunk angled backwards with his arms close to his body in a semi-defensive posture. Had there been a long pointed weapon in his hands I might well have mistaken him for a pikeman in a re-enactment of the battle of Edgehill.

A Renault saloon such as the one he was driving is an ergonomically designed, eco-friendly trend-setting motor, but when one is recklessly hurtling towards you with its driver's mind engrossed on something other than driving, then a different perspective of the car emerges. I tried to keep my cool as I approached him, my eyes fixed firmly on his. I decided to let him speak first. He was still in a sort of "no-man's-land" as far as the angle of his posture was concerned but it was no excuse for his stuttered words of, "Hiya, mate."

"Hiya mate" weren't quite the opening words I anticipated, it made it sound as though we had just recognised each other in one of the local pubs rather than an informal near-death meeting on a busy road.

Realising his error he did endeavour to make up for things and asked how I was. He then proceeded to call for an ambulance and we both sat on the side of the road in silence. I shook my head in disbelief as I heard the ambulance's siren sounding ever nearer. It had been a strange feeling waiting for it to arrive, as that day it seemed everyone and his dog had decided to commute into the city via this very roundabout. I was indeed the centre of attraction, and the Suzuki Bandit lying on its side on the roundabout's central plinth didn't escape the gaze of wide-eyed youngsters. I didn't realise I knew so many people. Come to think of it I didn't realise I knew so many strangers either but unfortunately these days one person's misfortune has a strange effect on the curiosity tendencies of another. Luckily I didn't suffer from any long-lasting effects, which was more than could be said about the bike. It was a write-off and I had to make the difficult decision as to whether to buy another. In the end as soon as the compensatory money came through, I decided to give it one more go.

One excursion I undertook, several miles away from my home to look at a 1970s Honda was particularly eventful. As the thing fired into life it made such a racket that it was an embarrassment to be in the vicinity. My younger daughter who hitherto had thought it might be novel to accompany me, soon decided to sit out in the car, whilst I tried to find something positive about a noisy pile of rust. In a short while the owner had disappeared under a haze of obnoxious fumes that pervaded the garage. The only reason I knew he was still there was because every now and again he would shout out that he was willing to drop the price by £20, and how would that suit me?

It wouldn't suit me at all well, as I wasn't into de-rusting chrome, touching up paintwork and degreasing motors, although I kept my thoughts to myself at this point. Soon it appeared I would get the thing for next to nothing, but I'd had enough. Thanking him for his time I came away empty handed.

The first bike I owned, before buying the Suzuki, was a small-engined Kawasaki. It had suited me well as regards travelling to work but as always when looking up reviews about things, (and I did this after the purchase) there was always someone who had had negative experiences. In this case there was some concern as the bike was belt driven. People had experienced belts snapping at seventy miles an hour. Because of this, it was always in the back of my mind. I'd let lorries and cars overtake me on occasions when travelling distances, rather than run the risk of them crashing into me should the belt break. I did however draw the line at tractors and push bikes.

Despite some reservations I did succumb to the charms of a Suzuki 500 after reading mostly good reviews. But being a biker was never quite the same. It was never easy avoiding roundabouts completely and I'm sure I often clocked up more miles than I needed to. A Ford Escort was purchased and the bike sold.

It was about this time that I was beginning to find my feet in the house, and was trusted with a mini excursion. The Tuesday club took place in a local hall and was reinstated after a short absence. The three residents in my house were biting at the chaff as they would soon meet up with like-minded friends. Initially I was more than happy to take them but when the other support workers approached me with smiles on their faces and seemed to go over the top with copious congratulations, I came to suspect a hidden agenda.

Nevertheless when the time came, with great excitement I bundled Anna, Cath and Dave into the car and off we went. When we arrived, one of the girls gave an excited cry, informing us karaoke was on the agenda that night. Several of the members had already put their names down to sing. Anna and Cath had to wait their turn but informed me that they had picked Cliff Richard's 'Summer Holiday' as their choice of song. I marvelled at their enthusiasm and waited with keen anticipation. Finally it was their turn to sing and a loud whooping was heard as I, and several of their friends, edged forward on our chairs. The girls looked confident as they gazed at the crowd that seemed to come from nowhere around them. I saw them ready for action as the first few bars sounded. There was understandable confusion for the first half minute as the girls looked to see which of them would start the singing first. As it turned out they started together, and I wasn't unduly disappointed when it soon became apparent that the only words they actually sang were 'summer' and 'holiday'. However nobody seemed to notice, and a loud applause greeted them on the last 'summer' and 'holiday'. The star of the show that evening was a lad who managed to find words to an instrumental that he had requested.

One lesson I picked up on when dancing with members of the Tuesday club, was always to keep an eye on your dance partner. I turned away for a few moments, during my first dance, then out of the corner of my eye I sensed some amusement directed towards me. Turning my head to face my partner I saw she had disappeared, I don't know how long I had been dancing on my own but it brought a smile to quite a few people's faces. Of course I made out that it was all part of the act but it was debatable whether I was believed.

I became enthralled with the evening's events whilst politely declining an invitation to partake in a spot of karaoke. As the evening drew to a close I sensed a climax building, as a hush went through the crowd, and an announcement was made concerning the next and last item on the agenda. It was the weekly raffle, for which my three residents had each bought numerous raffle tickets. Faces became serious as tickets were whipped out of pockets and laid out on the table. I noted the prizes were nothing too exotic. Perhaps a chocolate bar with a banana attached to it. My first thought was, well, if they don't win it wouldn't be much of a loss. Nothing could have been further from the truth, as their faces turned a strange reddish colour when someone else had the lucky ticket. One lad who won three chocolate bars and as a consequence three bananas, beamed with delight as he made his way back to his table, oblivious to the scowls on the faces of those who hadn't yet won. Luckily for us there were lots of prizes to be won, the organisers had obviously learnt the hard way, and all three of mine managed to win at least one prize. In the interests of the five-a-day guidelines I just hoped the bananas would be eaten, preferably during the next day, and not, under any circumstances, in my car.

One lady who had been a long-term resident in the house used to experience dramatic fits that resulted in a fall, usually when she was busying herself in the kitchen. The policy was one we found difficult to apply, but was absolutely necessary given the circumstances. We were to leave her completely alone, as she would fight us off if we tried to help her get to her feet. One of us had to then dash upstairs and lock ourselves in the loo. If we didn't do this she would bolt herself in there perhaps for twenty minutes or so. This could result in a very serious situation as we had no way of telling if she was alright or not. The first time I saw her crash to the floor my fellow worker, dashed upstairs and as per the policy locked herself in the loo. True to form Lucy picked herself up, and with alarming speed mounted the stairs and headed straight for the toilet. After frantically trying the toilet door for half a minute she admitted defeat and instead headed for her bedroom. We were able to keep an eye on her there, as somebody in their wisdom had removed the bedroom lock. I reflected that there couldn't have been too many assessments done where the sole intention was to prevent a vulnerable person from using the toilet.

I was asked to go on several training courses and one in particular was an eye opener. As there were over twenty of us in attendance, we were able to try scenarios that were not practical for a small group. One in particular that stood out was when we role-played. People in general tend to baulk at role-playing, but my last acting role as a shepherd during the school nativity play when I was five left me wanting more. I was obviously a frustrated actor, although my one and only line of "What shall we do?" was hardly Oscar material but my parents had said afterwards how impressed they were, even if they never mentioned it again. As, for whatever reason, there are a fair percentage of people who end up in a residential establishment and have few if any near relatives, we took it in turns to play that part. The idea was that the said person was surrounded by four people who represented their close relatives, then a ring further away, of those friends and acquaintances that they had made in the various homes or day centres. The third ring, which was the furthest away, represented the support workers, and other professional bodies who saw to their needs. When the first ring representing the family was removed, it was sadly apparent how lonely and confused it felt for the one in the middle. I was quite happy to attend meaningful courses such as this one and was pleased to take part in one that was well organised.

This brought to mind one of the first courses that I ever went on. I was in the middle of my four-year apprenticeship at my previous job and was selected, along with fifteen others, to attend a good communications course. The trouble with this was, that it was in a village hall and nobody had thought to organise transport, so we all turned up late, having had to go round cadging lifts. At the end of the day the trainer informed us he would see us again the following week. "See us next week?" we questioned in unison. When we told our managers that it was a three-day course they had signed us up to, they all declared they hadn't known this and threw a wobbly or two. We never got to complete our good communications course.

I was doing the rounds in various departments at the time and soon after this the head of department went missing. I sensed something was amiss due to several whispered conversations and it soon emerged that he had been dismissed. I noted that he often went home early. This was apparently to attend meetings with a firm that we did a lot of business with. One day his director rang the firm as he wanted to speak to the department head but they had never heard of him.

I wondered if the next department I would be assigned to would welcome me, as during my time with the previous one, the department head had absconded with one of his staff. I hoped I wouldn't be known as a catalyst in an act of instigating dodgy situations and ultimately making people disappear.

Another course that I attended was one basically focussing on self-defence. Again intriguing, but in a different way from any previous courses. An actor would come at us in an aggressive way and grab hold of our wrists or grip our shoulders tightly. We were shown techniques to counter this. I could well have done with going on this course several months previously. This was because I had registered with a care agency, for one week only, prior to my starting in my present employment. They had sent me to a residential home for children with behaviour problems and with no training or instructions, I had sat down with the residents at their evening meal. This was on my first day and my task was to help supervise them. One of the boys, about eleven years in age, was eyeing me menacingly. I wasn't sure how to take this and assumed that perhaps it was normal behaviour with some of the residents. Suddenly, seemingly out of nowhere, a knife flew through the air and missed me by inches. Still trying to take in the situation I was rooted to the spot when seconds later a fork was thrown in my direction. It was perhaps a good job he liked what was on his plate, otherwise that would have come my way too, (not that he now had any utensils with which to finish his meal). I think it was on the third day that another incident occurred which made me very respectful of my fellow workers. We had taken some of the boys to the white room, which was where they could chill out and relax. I identified with one of the bigger boys and although no words were exchanged, he was very smiley towards me. Suddenly he reached towards me and before I could move he had me in a headlock. Time seemed to stand still for a while, as my neck became more and more constricted. It's amazing what thoughts flash into your mind in situations such as this; it certainly wasn't one of the "bless him" variety. Relief came in the form of two other support workers who managed to prise him off. To be fair they tried to throw a positive slant on things. "It's not that he doesn't like you," one of my saviours stated, "He's done it before with people he gets on with," she added.

My response was also positive. "I appreciate what you are telling me, but I would be very much obliged if you could inform me, if ever you find out, that he has taken a big dislike to me."

Although I was only there a week, I felt an important piece of my learning puzzle had been put in place.

As the weeks went by I was given extra responsibilities and was prepared to work extra shifts in the guise of overtime. Most of the residents had somewhere to go, either at day centres, or other places that might constitute further education. During term time someone was needed to take them to their respective functions and I was that man, despite the early start. I particularly looked forward to taking them to the riding for the disabled facility where we got involved to a small degree. I say involved, it was more a case of following behind them as the horses alternated between walking and trotting, whilst we were expected to keep up. The horses were always led by a trainer so it wasn't imperative to keep pace but I always felt a failure if I didn't. It was rewarding to see the smiles on their faces. Animals can bring so much comfort to people, and horses specifically must be in the forefront of this.

The same however can't be said of donkeys, well, not in my experience least ways. Many years ago my grandparents thought it a nice gesture to hire a donkey from one of the seaside towns. These would be loaned out during the autumn months and there seemed to be a good uptake for these four-legged creatures. My younger brother myself and our cousins, waited impatiently for our turn to ride. I think I was fourth in line, which seemed the safest position to be in at the time, as the others would be the guinea pigs. What I didn't anticipate was the mood swings of an animal annoyed that it wouldn't now benefit from some much deserved out-of-season rest. Within a few seconds of my riding the beast, it seemed to have had enough of excitable children. From a sort of trotting speed it stopped abruptly and I tried hard to hold on to the saddle but to no avail, I hit the ground hard, swearing quietly to myself lest my mother was in hearing distance. Things didn't get much better, I think it threw all of us at various times. After my third fall I gave up on it, and rode my bike instead. I don't think the donkey people spend enough time in naming their donkeys; they should delve more into their character traits. The beast we had was called Lucky, which for us it clearly wasn't.

Often in an attempt to gain the residents' attention and generate a degree of interest in their social circle, I gave them titles which could be abbreviated. For instance if they helped me with one of the chores I would award them, verbally, the title of "personal helper" or PH, which I said they could use after their name. Or another one might be "secret helper", SH. This brought back a memory of my previous job, where I almost got into a spot of trouble. One apprentice whom I shall call JH was a popular worker but took things a bit seriously. He was hard working and seemed quite ambitious, so I told him we were thinking of rewarding him and would give him a promotion and a title to suit. He beamed enthusiastically as I awarded the honour of Trainee Works Advisory Technician to him. His face took a slightly different expression when I had to explain why other members of the office were laughing. "Whatever you do," I advised, "probably best not to use the acronym after your name."

I think karma caught up with me a few days later. I was asked to quote on a very elaborate cooling system as the more experienced engineer was on holiday. I studied the drawing that the clients had supplied, carefully thinking I had it sussed and even included a large contingency factor. However when the quote reached the clients they said they were amazed it was so low, and had we taken into consideration that besides the welding and fitting there was also a complicated machining operation that needed to be done. It's amazing how one's ego takes a battering after the obvious is pointed out. In the end one of our directors had to tell the client that we were unable to fulfil the contract. He refused to speak to me after that.

I believe karma followed me out into the car park after work. Walking to it, I noticed a car parked by the side of the road. The driver shouted that he'd broken down and could I give him a push. I put my sandwich box down on the grass verge and with the help of a colleague or two managed to get the car moving. I had anticipated a straightforward motion but the driver veered the car round to the right and much to some onlookers' amusement, mounted the grass verge and demolished my Tupperware sandwich box. The only grain of satisfaction I could glean from this was anticipating the expression of the driver's wife as she wondered, when the car pulled up on the drive, why a tuna mayonnaise sandwich which I hadn't had time to eat, was embedded in the tread of one of the tyres.

I wondered whether or not there was much more karma to be unleashed my way, and whether it would be compounded with past karma. I just hoped I wasn't Caligula in my last lifetime.

One of the residents decided that he no longer wished to be walked to his day centre; he wanted to go it alone. After much debate among the staff it was decided to let him walk on his own, but for the first few weeks one of us would follow him at a discreet distance. This decision wasn't taken lightly, as we weren't sure how he'd react if he spotted us, and what explanation could we possibly give? But in the interests of personal choice we were willing to grant his request. As I usually did the early shift I was one of the first to be the follower. I tried to ignore the funny looks on passing motorists' faces as I ducked behind a parked car every time Carl stopped and turned around. It wasn't so bad if the girls were doing the following, as one or two of them could probably have hidden behind a lamp post. With me, something more substantial was required. I was pleased when a Ford Transit passed by.

We had walked with Carl numerous times to his venue and had emphasised the traffic light system. He knew to wait until the green light was showing before he crossed. However as so often when a plan is formulated, there always seems to be one detail that one cannot predict. In this case Carl, following procedures exactly, was about to cross the road on green, when an ambulance with flashing lights and loud-sounding sirens approached. Luckily a tragedy was avoided as Carl had the sense to stay put and so we chalked it up as a resounding success, albeit with one modification to the health and safety policy.

One day I was sat in the office minding my own business when one of the staff burst in, and without seeming to draw breath, she informed me that Dave, one of our longer-term residents, had approached her with a request. It apparently involved me. The upshot was, would I go up with him in a four-seater plane at the local airfield? "It is after all his wish," came the parting shot. Had I let it slip during one careless moment that I expressed a moderate fear of flying? I decided to give her the benefit of the doubt nodding in a sort of agreement when she added, "Oh, by the way, he'd like to take control of the plane at some point during the trip." Normally this wouldn't have been too much of a problem but Dave unfortunately experienced several fits on a daily basis, despite the sheer amount of tablets that he was prescribed. The fits could last seconds or up to a couple of minutes in length. The day didn't exactly turn out to be the disaster I anticipated, apart from the worrying actions of the pilot who thought it fun to take pictures of Dave at the controls of the plane, and by turning around putting myself and Dave's mother in the frame. That said, photographs don't always turn out too successfully when the subjects have their eyes closed, and are wearing expressions of barely controlled fear. As anyone who has experience of this sort of jaunt knows all too well, you feel every slight twist and turn of the aircraft. More worryingly looking round, I didn't see a single parachute. However following a good landing, it reminded me, in retrospect, of the fun I had suppressed.

It was just after this that I managed to secure a second job. A 'Supporting People' organisation that I managed to impress during an interview were looking for another support worker. A male worker had handed his notice in and although nobody said as much, I got the impression that as the only male applicant I couldn't go too far wrong. All the same it was probably a close-run thing.

TWO

DOUG

In 2003, and several years before this time, the government subsidised councils nationwide with the primary aim of keeping as many people as possible in their homes, through the Supporting People scheme. We also had a carers' short break contract with the noble aim of giving the carer a break, up to three or four hours on average. This was achieved theoretically by taking out or at least looking after the person who was cared for. The first client I was assigned to, came through this latter contract, and his ideal preference was to play golf on a weekly basis. Doug was a complex character who liked to shock by coming up with a few carefully chosen swear words. It wasn't that

I hadn't heard the words, when the air turned blue; it was just that I hadn't heard them all used in the same sentence before. Still, golf was golf and although we only played on the local nine-hole course it was enough to satisfy both of us.

I had previously shadowed another support worker and all went well on both occasions. The first time I was due to be on my own with him, I decided to have a talk with his wife, to see if there were any problems I was likely to encounter. But it was apparent that Doug disliked being kept waiting. First of all the fidgeting started, followed by one or two barbed comments and when the looks bore into me it was time to go. We made sure he had enough money for the game, as I didn't want to explain to my new boss that besides paying for myself, I also had to pay for Doug due to his forgetfulness. Things actually got better after a few weeks in this respect as he offered to pay my golf fees. This impressed my boss no end. There were one or two occasions when I arrived that I was told he had gone missing. His wife had thought he was still somewhere in the vicinity, but after much calling we realised he was elsewhere. As it happened living a few miles outside of town, there weren't too many places for him to visit. I was able to find him relatively quickly by applying my tracking skills that I had gained at Cubs many years ago, despite missing out on the relevant badge for finding all twenty of the town's telephone boxes. Whether this was because of forgetfulness, or because of one innocent but apparently insensitive comment concerning

Akela made by one of my friends, I knew I should have distanced myself from him.

Fortunately Doug was quite agile so getting him in and out of the car was no trouble. The only problem he displayed in a physical sense was by way of connecting with the ball. He still had the power in his wrists to hit the ball a long way, but whether because of his condition, or because he had never been able to previously, he seemed unable to hit the ball in a straight line. It would invariably end up several degrees to the right. I had a similar problem except my ball, when I managed to connect, would end up several degrees to the left. In fact many a time we only saw each other, after the initial tee off, when we were both on the green. His usual opening comment after potting the ball was "How many did you take this time kid?" Why he called me "kid" I never knew, his eyesight didn't appear impaired. I knew this for a fact, as he possessed an uncanny knack of disappearing into the bushes after one of his slicing to the right shots, and come out smiling with two balls in his hand. Sometimes when our balls did land in the same vicinity he would select the one that was nearest to the green, even if it happened to be mine. I countered this to some extent by using a different colour ball to his. This worked well enough until I ran out of coloured balls; they seemed to prefer nestling in the middle of one of the many prickly bushes that were always in my way.

In answer to his questions as to quantity of shots I had taken, I usually answered truthfully. But however many I took, he always seemed to take one or two less. Even when I cheated he still seemed to have the better of me. I didn't mind too much as I was getting paid to play golf. When I told other golfers who happened to be around of this fact they must have thought that I was a professional, that is until I started sending clods of earth in their direction.

I did think it a bit mean that a course open to all and sundry would adhere, as far as I knew, to a sort of golf standard, as regards their par settings. I would look at the score card and exclaim in a slightly annoyed voice, "It says that this 250-yard hole is only par 3, surely that can't be right can it? I sometimes take three swipes just to connect with the ball."

"It is what it is kid," came the matter-of-fact reply. I looked at Doug and couldn't help but smile. I suppose when you make up your own score, you don't care what par the hole is. During all the time I played I believe I only ever achieved par three or four times. That is to say on individual holes, and not over the entire course. But what a feeling of ecstasy, akin to finding a matching pair of socks in one's small clothes drawer, sharing that same element of surprise and wonder. Or was it a feeling of sheer relief such as finishing a game of what I call Mr and for the present moment Mrs without falling out with one's other half, the memories of which still awaken the butterflies in my stomach. A friend had been in this unenviable situation when a family member had produced the game one evening. To make matters worse one of his questions took the form of, how did he rate his partner's navigational skills? This sort of inquisition would surely have tested the nerves of a saint. Three options presented themselves: bad, moderate or good. Thinking about it for as long as possible he ticked the moderate answer. This didn't go down at all well with his wife, who exploded in a display of indignation and sulked for the remainder of the game. I did ask him why he didn't lie to keep the peace. He replied that he had lied but not in the manner I had anticipated. Apparently what he should have selected was the word "bad".

Another problem I faced was Doug's lack of patience. Because it was a council-owned course, and only boasting nine holes, other not terribly good players like myself were often in front of us holding us up. Sometimes I had to step in front of Doug, thus preventing him from teeing off when there were other golfers attempting to escape, but were still not far enough away.

Doug's frenzied shouts to these fellow stragglers of, "Get out the fucking way you bastards" didn't always have the desired result.

On the whole, other golfers that we met on a more or less regular basis understood the problem and spoke to Doug as they would a friend and fellow golfer, even offering advice, which he subsequently ignored.

Sometimes we'd take an age to reach the green, usually when the ball ended up the wrong side of clumps of bushes. Trying to get round them or even over them could prove very frustrating. This wasn't exclusive to badly-hit balls; sometimes we'd take an age when everything should have been okay. I'd played golf before a fair few times when I was younger. My father had been treasurer to a local club and also possessed a good set of clubs. These were the ones I was playing with currently, having inherited them after my father passed away. Not that a good set of golf clubs makes one a good golfer as I knew only too well. He hadn't been the best of golfers; in fact I don't think he'd had a proper handicap even. He was better at bowls, and like father like son, I found myself struggling to play a reasonable round of golf. It was just a shame Doug thought bowls was beneath him.

Another area of frustration was when we turned up at our usual time of around 9.15, only to find a seniors' tournament going on. Although they started much earlier than this, and depending on how many were participating, there were still a few queuing up to play when we arrived. These tournaments seemed to be organised randomly as far as I could see. I suppose we could have planned ahead •but I had allotted a set time and day to take him out, and it was difficult to change things. Doug seemed to have more patience with this scenario, going as far as offering some advice and amusing one-liners.

I can only recollect one near miss with a golf ball and that was when I had just emerged from a bush, surprisingly with my ball in hand. As I stood to my full extent, a ball whistled over my head missing me by a few inches. A strong-looking lad with a very red face was full of apologies. It later transpired that he was a very good golfer and could easily hit the ball over 250 yards. I looked out for him after this. On one occasion we heard a bit of a commotion. We had noticed that two lads whom we hadn't seen before were in front of us as we approached the fourth tee. The tee off was nearest to the entrance and it was evident that the two had sneaked onto the course without paying. Luckily for me, it hadn't registered with Doug that this was the case, until two older golfers who happened to be nearby and noticed the incident remonstrated with the lads.

"It's lucky I didn't see them first," was Doug's reaction. "I would have reported them to their mothers, they wouldn't try that stunt again after that." I may have been wrong but I could see two flaws in his reasoning. Reporting lads to their mothers probably didn't have the same impact that it once did and besides which, were they, under Doug's intense interrogation, meekly going to divulge the whereabouts of their mothers? I decided to say nothing and the incident was resolved when the two lads left the course with fleas in their ears. It got me thinking about other subjects that lose impact over time. For instance, I was quite proud of my five O levels achieved through hard slog in the sixties, especially as one of them was Physics. Nowadays however youngsters are boasting GCSEs too numerous to remember in subjects I've never even heard of. With that in mind I decided not to include my CSE in Geography in my short list of achievements.

After two or so years the funding ran out for Doug and the last I heard he was hoping for a member of his family to take him out. In all of the time that I took Doug out, we only had to abandon our golf session on one occasion. The rain was extremely heavy that day. He asked if we could go and see his sister and directed me to a house not too far away from the course. We walked in through the back door, he settled himself down and made us both a cup of coffee. We were there for perhaps an hour before we left. I always assumed it was his sister's house although we never actually got to lay eyes on her, that day or any other. I didn't ask too many questions just in case. I said goodbye to Doug after our last game of golf and never saw him again.

THREE

LESLEY

I had heard of Lesley through some amusing anecdotes told by some of the other support workers. Apparently three hours was never enough, especially when shopping was involved, which it invariably was. Shopping trips were not really in the Supporting People's agenda, but in Lesley's case, guidelines were waived due to her vulnerability when dealing with finances. Again I was introduced to her through another support worker. As she lived in the country it had been set up for us to use her car for trips to save using our own. Although only in her mid-fifties, she was unable to drive due to restricted vision and restricted mobility. The first problem I encountered was that she was unable to make up her mind as to which town we should be visiting that day. I would perhaps drive 100 yards or so and on approaching the T junction that would determine our destination she would still be dithering.

"I can't make up my mind whether to go to Ledbury or Malvern," she would state in a broad West Country accent. Eventually we would end up at one of the two places, but often a disjointed version of "Eeny meeny miny moe" would dictate events.

Banking visits were an eye opener. We would queue up to see how much money was in her account. She would study the bank statement, mumbling that someone had been at her money, and always seemed surprised that the care agency was the culprit, even though it was in a legitimate capacity. She would then sit down wondering whether she should draw out fifteen or twenty pounds. Then we would queue up again and draw out the requisite amount of money, then off shopping and the marathon began. Lesley was able to walk a moderate distance unaided, certainly enough to get her round the shops. If we ended up in her preferred town we'd start off in the local butcher's shop. As the proprietors knew her well they usually had prepared a few nice cuts of meat, and as such the time spent in the shop was relatively short. We were always well received and the cost never seemed to vary too much from week to week, I suspect this was to negate the, "Is that the best you can do?" question.

The next shop along the street was the florists. Here we could spend an age. Although there may have not been too much choice, there was enough for Lesley to ponder. On one occasion the shopkeeper had tested us by displaying one pot of four small pansies, and an adjacent pot with three larger pansies nestling in the soil. We were standing outside despite the weather not being the best on the day, and as the pavements were narrow we were constantly having to shuffle about to allow people to pass. Picking both pots up, one in each hand, Lesley endeavoured to see which one showed the petals off to best effect. When she failed to establish that, she turned them around in the hope that one display might outshine the other from the top. I thought at one point that she was about to tip the pots totally upside-down in an endeavour to see if anything could be gleaned that way, but she thought better of it. Twenty minutes later she appeared to have reached a decision and grabbing the pot with four pansies in, walked into the shop. Unfortunately on the way in she knocked the pot against a shelf and one of the petals fell off.

"I suppose you want the other pot now," came the slightly annoyed voice of the proprietor.

Lesley looked a bit puzzled before replying, "Actually I've changed my mind thanks, perhaps next week I'll look at some more." With that she walked out of the shop, and without daring to look back I followed suit.

I always dreaded the times when one of her relatives had a birthday because that meant a trip to the card shop. One such visit took longer than usual mainly because of the thoughtless but well-meaning intention of the shopkeeper.

We pored over countless cards with varying sentimental messages, although my opinions were quickly discarded, despite, "What do you think of this?" type questions. I couldn't stop myself from clock watching as every card was picked up, felt for thickness, read three times and compared to the price of the previous card. Eventually she decided on one, only for the shopkeeper to announce that he had just received another box of cards which he hadn't had time to put out. And did she want to look through it?

The last shopping trip was to the supermarket, which sometimes surprisingly enough was the quickest of our excursions. I suspected this was due to tiredness on her part, not to mention the tiredness on my part. The sprouts were scrupulously examined and only the best were put into the bag, as were the potatoes. Although said sprouts appeared the next week on the kitchen table, untouched and looking much the worse for wear. I wasn't surprised we rarely had to purchase tea bags as she was into saving the environment, in that one tea bag could refresh two people. Lesley was always happy to make me a cup of tea and offer me a biscuit or two on our return to her home. I can remember an occasion when another support worker, who was shadowing me, was surprised when the teabag that had been shared between Lesley and myself ended up in her cup.

There were dental appointments that we attended on a fairly regular basis and as often happens in a busy practice there were often long waits to see a dentist. Lesley decided to fill in the time by recounting certain village scandals. This was quite an amusing distraction for me. The impending trouble was, other patients were always in earshot and we were never sure if one or other of them was connected to people in these village revelations. Even the son of one of the dentists came in for a bit of flack. Apparently he had been a bit wild in his youth before settling down. He also happened to be working in the practice and was often walking past us during our wait. At times, when Lesley was reminded of some anecdote when he was in the vicinity, I was praying that perhaps he was hard of hearing. Whether or not he was I doubt it very much, but I hope he was able to turn a deaf ear to a lonely lady's whims.

Lesley did have underlying health problems, which sometimes caused breathing difficulties. On one visit I sensed she wasn't feeling too well as she was very quiet and confused. She suddenly requested that I take her to the city hospital some fifteen miles away. She couldn't get down the steps of her bungalow but with the help of several telephone directories piled on top of one another, I eventually got her into the car. It was fair to say that Lesley's sense of direction was different from mine. She gave way when I insisted on the main road but when we got within four miles of the hospital she insisted on going the long way round, via the outskirts. By this time she was suffering badly and I really wanted to go the quickest way. The trouble was when I argued the case she became more agitated and so I arrived ten minutes later than I intended to. I pulled up in the car park and within minutes she had two doctors attending to her, as she sat in the car. She was hospitalised at once. The following week I was told that she had been transferred to a cottage hospital nearer her home and could I drive to her house, transfer to her car then collect her from the said hospital? When I arrived at the hospital reception area I was halfway through explaining who I was and wondering whether I was in the right building when I heard a nurse shouting, "When are you going to get out of this bloody bath Lesley? I've got other things to do you know." I realised at once that I had come to the right place. She had made a full recovery and I drove her home that day after the usual bank, butcher and florist visit.

Occasionally we spent the afternoon and more in attending her parents' grave. It meant, of course buying the flowers first. On one occasion we went from village to village before finding suitable bunches, as she seemed to like buying enough for several pots. The first fifteen minutes after having arrived at the churchyard, she had the flowers placed to her satisfaction. The next twenty minutes saw the flowers rearranged, then rearranged again until they were totally at odds with the first arrangement. Eventually the flowers were laid out to her satisfaction and I would invariably breathe a long sigh of relief. Now and again she would glance at me in an apologetic way and once when we had overshot her allocated time, even said, "I hope I'm not keeping you too long."

I responded immediately, "Well I did mention that I had to be on time today."

"I can't remember you saying that, perhaps you should have spoken in a louder voice," was the reply to end all protestations.

It might be that someone in the near future will devise an app whereby in the comfort of your own home you can play around with flowers selectively chosen from the florist's stock via photos on their website. These can then be superimposed onto photos, as in this case, of the gravestone of a loved one. This would have saved me a considerable amount of time but I doubt whether it would be half as much fun though, but some sort of computerised interaction whereby one could view a card shop's entire stock of birthday cards might just swing it for me.

We would sit on occasions for a long time outside her childhood home, now owned by complete strangers, staring up at the windows as she reminisced. I could empathise with this, as often people without too much of a future will revert back to childhood memories. Although I often arrived home late after our sessions, who could resist a shared teabag and a slightly suspect Digestive?

I did miss her warmth, her geniality and despite her health issues, her positive outlook on life, when I was put to work in a different area of the county.

FOUR

THOSE WİTH A VİSUAL İMPAİRMENT (AND THE ODD FAUX PAS)

I have always admired, even held in great esteem, those who make the most of their time on earth despite their visual impairment. An ex-colleague told me of an incident which he would never forget. At the start of the Second World War he was a child, and one evening during the blackout he found himself in a very unfamiliar part of Birmingham in a pea souper fog. He was Crying as he walked past a public house, which didn't go unnoticed by a man exiting the pub. When asked why he was crying, the boy told him of his situation. The man after being told the boy's address told him to follow and off they set. My colleague noted that the man didn't put a foot wrong, and twenty-five minutes later they arrived at his front door. It was only as the man was walking away that the boy realised he had been taken home by a person who was blind.

MIKE

Mike, a visually impaired client in his forties whom I would support from time to time, was very animated on one of my visits. He held up a wad of photographs for me to peruse, and declared that although he wasn't able to make them out, he had made contact via an online dating agency, and what did I think of his potential date? The first two photographs were of a beautiful girl in her twenties with long blonde hair and an enchanting smile. I couldn't help but remark that he was indeed lucky and should take up the lady's offer of their meeting. That seemed to decide it for him and he vowed there and then to make contact. As I went down through the pile of photos I discerned a lady in her fifties. "Homely" was the best description that came to mind and certainly not in the same beauty class as the younger girl. The penny dropped when Mike remarked that amongst the photos there were some pictures of the lady's daughter. I didn't have the heart to tell him of my mistake. I believe the subsequent relationship wasn't too long lasting.

I did greatly admire Mike who had no vision whatsoever, but nothing stood in his way when determined to travel all over the world in his quest to attend concerts and other events. The only slight negative I experienced with Mike was when I had to meet him at the local supermarket. I was never sure of the time-scale he could be allotted. It all depended on whether he was short of tinned food or not. If he was, I would start off by picking up two or three different cans of peaches. He would shake each one in turn then ask if there were any more makes he could try out. I wasn't sure whether he was feeling for quantity or even quality but something must have clicked when he gave a loud exclamation of success. A casual observer some distance away must have wondered why Morrisons were allowing someone to play the maracas in their store. He did seem to be enjoying himself, in fact had I not had my name badge on I might just have joined in. My professional identity kept me from doing so.

BiLL

Bill was referred to us by the Royal National College for the Blind. He had asked if there was any way he could be assisted with computer technology, as his visual impairment was such that he wasn't even able to discern changes of light patterns. I wasn't sure if I was the right person to assist in this way but on expressing my concern, it was agreed that one of the girls who was extremely suitable but was unable to make weekly visits would alternate with me. I travelled to one of the northerly towns in the county one Wednesday afternoon, found the street after a few wrong turns, and knocked on the door of a spacious and pleasant-looking bungalow. A lady in her sixties answered, informed me my office had confirmed my visit by telephone, and ushered me into her front room. I was introduced to her husband who was in the doorway of an adjoining room. I was amazed at how steady he seemed as he negotiated a coffee table and easy chair to make his way over to me. The wife made a cup of tea whilst I got to know her husband. I had heard that people who lose their sight tend to compensate somewhat by strengthening their other senses but was still amazed as to his non-visual awareness. He seemed to know exactly where the teacup was in relation to his wife's hands. Matters took another curious turn when he stood up, glanced at the newspaper that was on the coffee table and deposited it into the magazine rack. I was beginning to wonder if he was playing a game; surely he wouldn't be so blatant as to falsify his condition and how could I pretend to be helpful when I suspected that he was giving us the runaround? I half expected him to challenge me to a game of darts. I decided as this was just an introductory visit I would leave and report my suspicions to my manager. As I was leaving I informed the couple that I would alternate weekly visits with one of the girls. They looked at me in utter surprise and for a while they found themselves tongue tied before the wife blurted out, "What, to mend the fire alarm?"

"Fire alarm?" I repeated.

"Yes, we were expecting someone to come and rectify ours, it keeps giving false alarms."

It was my turn to sound surprised. "This is no. 29 Larkrise Drive, isn't it?"

"No, we're no 31, 29 is next door."

"But the bin outside your door?" I tried to salvage some respectability.

"The bin men aren't always careful when it comes to relocating the bins," came the retort. "We've had to swap with number 37 before now."

Making my apologies, I hurried out and knocked on their neighbours' door. Bill's wife looked at her watch as I entered, another set of apologies was forthcoming before I settled down with yet another cup of tea. Bill was quite a character and despite his visual impairment was keen to learn all he needed to know on his talking computer. He had taken several photographs on his digital camera and was keen to edit the best ones. His goal was to create a variety of cards using his photographs as the focal point. Over the weeks we had various successes not to mention one or two failures, but all the while Bill was keen to use his best shots and for us to edit them, especially with regard to tone and definition. He was obviously a perfectionist and despite his condition everything had to be of the best quality, as confirmed by myself and Bill's wife. I would describe the scene as fully as I could and attempt to hype them up to a level that the photos told a story. Unfortunately Jess who was meant to visit alternately with me was taken ill, and never actually got to meet Bill. I did what I could but when the Royal National College for the Blind rang to say that they now had a suitable support worker, I relinquished my visits in order for them to take over.

FIVE

GERRY

Gerry was referred to us by a social worker. He was a retired ex-vicar and although living in a secure bungalow, he was struggling to live independently. It was suggested that we apply through the social care system for a care package. Initially however I was tasked with ensuring he was able to cope as best he could, which chiefly involved various aspects of looking at domestic aids, and looking at his paperwork in general. One of the first problems I encountered was in the guise of a rather unfriendly cat. I found out just how unfriendly it was the first time I bent over to stroke it. A vicious paw shot out and I just managed to pull my hand away before too much blood was lost.

"Oh I should have told you," was Gerry's reaction. "He doesn't take kindly to people who are new to him. Last week he had a go at the postman as he pushed my post through the letterbox."

First action plan I verbally noted was to get a postbox installed outside, well away from vicious paws. My boss became another victim of Gerry's furry companion. She had planned a visit to ensure that the action plan that was devised was firmly understood. Soon after the visit she was able to add, as soon as her hand had healed, another item to her risk assessment. I hadn't thought to warn her; my excuse afterwards was, "Well I didn't think it would do that as it did seem settled on its reclining cushion." As my boss let herself in, as pre-arranged, she thought it fitting to announce herself by putting her head through the kitchen/lounge hatch. Without warning the cat shot across the room and attached its claws to her blouse. Trying to put a brave face on matters she feigned a look of nonchalance, pretended it was just a mild inconvenience and asked how Gerry was feeling. She mumbled a few other pleasantries as she tried to fight off sharp claws and if I can remember rightly, teeth as well. I was amazed at her tenacity. She must have stuck it out for a good thirty seconds before withdrawing from the hatchway and breaking the hold that the cat had on her. She reappeared a minute or two later wearing a strange countenance, a mixture of pain and professionalism but with watchful eyes darting from side to side.

As part of the action plan there were times when we had to shop and attend medical appointments. I was reminded to direct Gerry to the most suitable and easy to open items when buying cans of soup and domestic cleaning products. I probably wasn't the best at advising people in this respect as I sometimes had to get the kids to open various pots and lids, especially those deemed as being child proof. I would have to learn fast. It was a matter of life and death if we didn't make sure the cat was well fed. Woe betide the unacceptable situation that we would return home with no cat food. Whether or not it was my imagination, it seemed to regard us suspiciously as we unpacked his shopping.

It had been arranged that I would drive Gerry's car. This was one of the heaviest of the 1970s saloons and to add to the problem, it usually took me a full minute to reverse it out of the garage. This was mainly due to a temperamental gearbox, although to be fair I wasn't exactly the best of drivers when it came to reversing larger vehicles. It didn't help that I had to go through several dummy gear changes before reverse was engaged. The appearance of the car looked unlike any other designs of the day, in short it reminded me of Dracula's coach. Gerry lived about six miles from the city centre and although he struggled to walk at times he could climb into the passenger seat unaided, but the situation we found ourselves in one afternoon tested both of our nerves. We approached the centre of the city on an inner ring road, having just negotiated a roundabout and were on the inside lane of a dual carriageway, when the ignition cut out and the car rolled quickly to a stop. A car behind sounded its horn as the driver swerved to avoid us; others followed suit. Quickly assessing the situation it was worrying to say the least, as Gerry would struggle to exit the car and besides there was little room for escape. The city's ancient wall was less than a metre away. It was only a matter of time before someone would run into the back of us. As more cars shot past, a voice in my head seemed to say, "I'd get out and push if I were you."

Gerry thought I was going to leave him to his fate as I stepped out of the car but with one hand on the steering wheel, and the other pushing against the door jamb, I moved the car inch by inch towards a pull-in about thirty yards in front of us. I had no idea how long this took but I got to safety in the end, and even parked the car in some sort of order. Had the producers of *The World's Strongest Man* been watching me pushing a one-ton plus car, with an eighteen-stone passenger in, I probably would have been put into the final in an instant. What was more impressive was the fact that the final twenty yards were on a slope. Was this an unseen helping hand at force here bearing in mind that Gerry was an ex-vicar, or was this a case of a powerful surge of adrenaline on my part? Mechanics were called and we found ourselves riding home in a pickup truck.

The following week threw another puzzling slant on the situation and set my mind reeling for answers. We had the car back from the mechanics the day before I picked Gerry up. They assured us that they had fixed the problem and had replaced a blown fuse. We were on our way to town but hadn't gone more than two miles when the car cut out again. Undaunted I stepped out of the car, and flexed my muscles knowing I had total command of the situation. Although we were on a straight piece of road I decided to move us along a few yards where the road was wider. My consternation was apparent as despite applying all my strength to the door jamb, the car wouldn't budge an inch. Gerry suggested I take the hand brake off; sheepishly I bent down and reached over, but immediately realised it wasn't on. Before he could suggest I look to the gear stick I quickly checked this too, but found it to be in neutral. I tried moving the car again but to no avail. On phoning some new mechanics as we had lost confidence in the previous ones, we didn't have too long to wait before they came to our aid. The next day I rang them and told them of the previous breakdown and my get out of trouble push. At first they thought I was having them on as it had taken two of them some time and effort to push the car into the garage after releasing it from the pickup truck. This was a collective four-hand push from the rear of the car and not a one-handed push, as I had done with the other hand on the steering wheel. The car broke down one more time before it was repaired for good, and coincidently rolled to a stop directly outside the house of one of the mechanics.

Another trip into town turned into another highly emotional time. Through one of my previous jobs as an engineer, collectively I experienced quite a few negative issues. I suppose in all the years I was there it was inevitable. One of the most frustrating aspects was the relationship with the firm's hierarchy. As a trained engineer a previous boss had sought my opinion when it came to buying machines and specialised tooling. Mutual respect was paramount, as it should be if an employee is made to feel important. However when he left, a new boss was promoted over me and although some degree of respect was mutual we disagreed on several engineering issues. Had he been trained as an engineer I might have given way somewhat, but he had been trained in a totally different field. A new metal forming machine had been purchased without my having any involvement or even knowledge. It subsequently proved difficult to operate and true to form I was given the task of sorting it out. This was just one of a number of issues. Another major source of annoyance was when another engineer was employed, ostensibly on the same grade as myself but paid a colossal lot more. And why did I only receive a barometer after thirty years of hard slog and toil, whilst others ended up with golf clubs or other sports equipment?

Now I was free of the place, I had often thought of what I might say if ever I came across my old boss, and there he was, walking straight towards me in the women's hygiene aisle of the local supermarket. The problem was, I was pushing Gerry who was in the supermarket's wheelchair and John, my ex-boss, was with his wife and baby daughter. All my premeditated thoughts whirred around in my brain; this was my big chance to say my piece. I looked at Gerry, then John and his wife, then I noted their shopping trolley and blurted out in a moment of panic, "My what a hungry baby you have." John and his wife laughed politely, Gerry laughed politely, John and his wife walked away, Gerry asked to go to the delicatessen. I, discounting the baby in my calculations, although she may have had a chortle or two, was the only one who didn't laugh, politely or otherwise. My big chance was gone, never to return as John and his family moved away shortly after this.

It wasn't really John that I had an issue with, it was the system, and especially it seems that which is typical of many engineering firms. Often, as in the firm I worked for, the hierarchy usually consisted of non-engineering personnel. Directors especially it seemed to me were sales and/or office based people who had risen up through the ranks. These people had to delegate engineering problems to others that they trusted, but then again they weren't necessarily the best ones to find solutions, and quite often engineering projects and decisions fell flat because of a lack of engineering skills.

The firm I had worked for previously were a subsidiary of a larger organisation whose three-lettered name ended in the word Press. In an endeavour to appear benevolent, the hierarchy at Press came up with an idea that they thought would show off the professionalism and pride of the workers. They decided that if an employee had been with them for ten years or more they deserved some sort of recognition. The men were to receive a tie with the word "Press" printed over it, whilst the women were given a brooch with the same word proudly displayed. Unfortunately one unsavoury incident, whereby a male employee took advantage of the word displayed on the bosom of one of the women, led understandably, to one of a series of complaints. At least things were nipped in the bud before more instances of a similar kind were reported. The brooches were returned en mass and women's modesty was restored.

Sorting out a care package for Gerry was never going to be a quick affair. People had to be interviewed; references had to be sought and a separate bank account had to be set up in order to deal solely with the care package money. All this took time but eventually a lady was selected. She was hard working and reliable and initially everything went smoothly. However Gerry was an individual who missed supporting others. Retirement didn't come easy, his wife had passed away several years ago and his only child, whom he brought up single-handedly, had married, and although living not too far away was busy with a stressful job and a large family to support. As far as I can make out it seems vicars on retirement were discouraged from settling too close to the parish that they once served. This was to smooth out the path for the new vicar. It was felt that some members of the congregation might be tempted to bypass the replacement vicar by going to the previous one on certain spiritual matters. So although Gerry knew the area well, as he had worked in the vicinity in a previous posting, most of his friends and acquaintances were elsewhere. Also because of his physical problems he wasn't able to volunteer his services and having to rely on others only emphasised a source of frustration. In an apologetic moment he dismissed his carer, and once again I had to call in social services, this time to sort out the money allocated to his care account.

In between the various meetings we decided to visit a local park that I knew had a buggy, which could accommodate someone with mobility issues. It was about the same size as a golf buggy, whereby the driver and passenger could sit side-by-side. It was also spacious enough for a walking frame to fit in the back. A map of the route was given to us, which I rolled up and put in my back pocket. I had been through the parkland countless times and obviously didn't need a map. We'd done two laps of the circuit on this warm spring day. It was as though every plant and tree was bursting into life following a protracted winter. Feeling full of confidence and joy, I decided to veer off the official route and take an alternative path. This would have been okay under normal circumstances but unfortunately it had been raining quite heavily the few days before and it wasn't long before I realised my mistake. We came to a bank that I'd walked up several times with my family, but it hadn't seemed quite so steep then and certainly not so muddy as far as I could remember.

Suddenly it appeared in front of us, teasing, even daring us to mount. The buggy, despite my acceleration, came to a halt at an angle to the bank. I turned round and was about to apologise to Gerry and ask him if he would mind stepping off the buggy whilst I tried to sort out the mess I had gotten us into. As it happens I didn't have to ask him, as due to the position of the buggy he was almost out of it anyway. Letting go of its side he somehow managed to clamber out and hung onto a branch, whilst I thought through the situation. Unable to move the buggy any further I managed to push it away from the bank onto another path. This initially was hidden to me, and although not on the main route was less steep and less muddy. With the help of his walking frame he managed to follow me up to the safe path. He was in pensive mood on the way back home for some reason, but being the person he was, when his voice resurfaced he spoke about the incident in a matter-of-fact sort of way. I did however detect a cunning hidden message which seemed to say "try not to do that again please". As fate would have it I didn't have much longer with Gerry; he died quite quickly after being admitted to hospital. Although our sessions were often dramatic, sometimes strenuous but mostly enjoyable, I always believed he couldn't wait to join his wife in the spirit world. I didn't dare ask what became of the cat, and I didn't hang about when the will was read, just in case it was destined to be left in my care.

SIX

PAUL

Paul was in his late sixties when we first supported him. He had lived in a village most of his life and always had a good story to tell. He had been divorced quite some time before we got involved. Initially he was with another support worker, but over the years I got to know him through illness or holiday cover. When the Supporting People and its replacement contract came to an end I tended to his shopping needs on a private basis. His paperwork was of concern and it soon became apparent that he received no pension despite his entitlement to it. This was rectified after numerous phone calls. Over the years various improvements to his flat were carried out although it was still short of what I would consider as exuding that homely feel; when one is renting as he was, sometimes compromises have to be met. When I supported him privately he had had a serious infection and it was necessary for him to have a right leg amputation. The flat being downstairs and suitable for wheelchair use was no barrier to his continuing to live there, but it was still recommended that he have a prosthetic leg fitted, so between myself and his other support worker we ferried him alternately back and forward to the relevant clinic.

Encouraging as we were, he couldn't get on with the false leg. It was never going to work. It either chafed his thigh or it fell off altogether. It was cumbersome to put on and to take off, and whilst he could manage to get into a car, that was all he wanted. The false leg was discarded and he relied on us, his support workers, more and more. This was okay with me but one of the obstacles I encountered was his dog, who took a dislike to me. I was told it wasn't personal although Charlotte, his other support worker, seemed to hit it off with this wiry terrier. Having been bitten by a dog when I was young didn't help my relationship with animals. Also I had my fair share of bites since then, so perhaps I should have been used to it. Harmless-looking hamsters took great delight in sharpening their teeth on the bones of my fingers. On more than one occasion I wondered if I could get away by accidentally letting them escape, in the interests of enabling them to live naturally so to speak. Even the two rabbits we acquired proved a handful. They fought and scratched their way through life until the hutch which I had painstakingly constructed in the days before I knew about power tools, looked like something out of Jurassic Park after the dinosaurs had been let loose. We even had to get a friend to cut their nails as our attempts met with contempt, as far as the rabbits were concerned. In the end they were returned to the seller on the condition she had what remained of the hutch.

Paul came to a solution as far as the dog was concerned. He would shoo the dog outside the kitchen door immediately after I arrived, then get into the wheelchair and push himself out. Meanwhile it was my duty to let the dog know I was in the flat by calling him from the hallway that led into the kitchen. The dog would rush in from outside, barking the neighbourhood down, and head straight towards me. Luckily there was a swinging stable door between the hall and kitchen that was an obvious barrier, when Paul remembered to bolt it, but often the dog's head would appear over the top of this stable door. I was amazed at how high he could jump as he seemed determined to sink his teeth into any part of my body he could reach. I just hoped he wasn't clever enough to devise a way to pole vault over the door. Although should this happen, *Britain's Got Talent* may have been interested. As soon as Paul felt the dog was safely ensconced he would lock the back door and wheel himself to join me at the front of the house. Prior to our trips into town he would use his wheelchair to get himself adjacent to the front of the car, remove the right-hand side frame and lever himself with a lurching motion, which seemed to throw him sideways into the car seat. I always had my heart in my mouth whilst he did this as trying to pick someone up who had fallen was a no-no. Once in town we would pull up at the local supermarket and sit in an outside cafe that allowed smoking, whilst waiting for the bank to open. The supermarket visit was the final chore of the day before the process of transferring back into my car was carried out.

I never liked talking about one of my hobbies to people who, even if they weren't interested, couldn't participate due to their disabilities. However I'd come across a deserted cottage on one of my walks around the village and I knew Paul would know something about it. The cottage intrigued me because it had a tree growing up through one of the rooms. To get to it the former occupants must have needed a four-by-four and even then it would have been a heart-in-the-mouth sort of journey. Also it was in the middle of a wood and although the estate apparently occupied three acres, there was hardly an open area whereby vegetables could be grown. It transpired that a large family had lived there and over the years they had left, one by one, either by their own volition or via the undertakers, until there was just one elderly son left. The cottage had no electricity or running water but I did make out an old gas canister sticking out of the broken-down front door. Paul told me of the time John the son used to walk down to the pub in the village to join him and the other pub regulars. He had an interesting lift home at times, especially after lock-ins, and presumably an excess of a certain beverage. This erred on the dangerous side, and was not to be recommended these or any other days. Whether going home in the bucket of a dumper truck is deemed legal or not is anybody's guess but being tipped from it outside his front door probably wasn't. On John's death, the house was put up for sale but it was a long time before it was bought and it took an even longer time for the new owners to knock the old cottage down and construct a new one.

Paul's health took another downward turn as another infection materialised. He had a difficult choice to make as the hospital had said in no uncertain terms that unless he had his remaining leg removed, they couldn't guarantee he would survive much longer. To make matters worse, if that were possible, he would have to agree to employ a cleaner and give up his dog, although whether this could be enforced I doubted very much. His other support worker was given the task of sorting this out. After many changes of mind he agreed to these terms and I agreed, with misgivings, to continue taking him into town. Being very inventive Paul thought of a way of getting into the front seat of my car. Again he pulled up in his wheelchair adjacent to the door, pushed his body up with both hands, transferred one hand onto the car seat and pushed with his other hand, thus shuffling over onto the car seat. I had suggested a banana board whereby he would slide himself along from wheelchair to car seat but he wouldn't have this. He'd say things to the effect that banana boards were for people who were severely disabled. Did he not think that having no legs might just fall into this category? To safeguard myself I did have to get him to sign a form to the effect that I wouldn't be held responsible for any mishaps.

His life didn't actually change much due to the second amputation. A cleaner was employed then subsequently dismissed as not needed. The dog, which had been given away, had subsequently bitten its new owner and was returned without any fuss to Paul. This meant I still had to go through the motions of distracting the dog, which seemed even more aggressive than normal. A telephone call one evening had me wondering what was amiss, as he requested an extra visit from me the following day. When I arrived I was confronted with a 250-litre aquarium complete with five Gourami and several other tropical fish. I had told him some time back that I kept a small aquarium so he was enlisting my help. Against recommendations he had put the fish in the tank two or three days after its purchase. The good bacteria hadn't had time to build up to render the ammonia produced by the fish harmless. This action could prove fatal, but he seemed to have got away with it. With the help of his neighbour and a local aquarium store, he had got what he wanted. A fortnight later he had purchased another 250-litre aquarium, this time for fish that didn't require heating, such as goldfish. A fair few visits to the aquarium shop were made after the supermarket visit. We looked at and he subsequently bought two mobility scooters, the smaller one for short journeys and a much larger one for longer journeys, which he bought from a former client who had no need for it.

As the village was fairly self-sufficient and possessed a butcher's shop, a corner shop, along with a pub, he was able to get by. Unfortunately he was discouraged from drinking at the pub, as not being able to get up the steps to the pub itself, he had a habit of asking complete strangers before they walked in to fetch him his drinks. It was unfortunate as most people didn't seem to mind but the management thought it inappropriate.

I enjoyed my visits to Paul but one day I had the inevitable text. A next-door neighbour had found him motionless in his bed; he had passed away. He was buried next to his mother's grave in the village. At the subsequent wake I met up with some of his ex-workers and colleagues of mine.

SEVEN

ANDY & GEORGE

Andy was referred to us by his specialist nurse due to his degenerative disorder of the nervous system. If anyone deserved a four-hour carer's break it was his mother, as Andy's condition was of the worst type and had progressed into a degenerative neurologic state. I had to reassure him on occasions that the aliens he saw sitting next to him were something only he could see, for whatever reason. Perhaps as they appeared friendly enough they could be there to reassure him. Or if he could manage to regard them as harmless visitors then at the very least they shouldn't bother him too much. Another disconcerting aspect was the fact that he was unable to express himself as he wished. His condition caused him to stutter or to be more precise, words stuck in his throat almost as though he didn't have the strength to complete the last syllable. He had a quiet voice anyway, and it was difficult to pick up his concerns at the best of times.

His father had left home some time before and there was an obvious issue with this but I never did ascertain the full truth. We got on famously as we found common interests. Before Andy, I had briefly supported George, another man who lived with the same condition, so was prepared for certain eventualities. For instance George had requested a visit to a nearby castle, complete with its own vast parkland. In my enthusiasm I had suggested we go to the main attraction, which happened to be what I assumed was a moderately easy-to-solve maze. Unknown to me at the time, the symptoms of his condition were made worse when the client encountered confined spaces, and ultimately mazes fell into this category. We were okay for five minutes as I prattled on about various things, but as we went past the same bench half a dozen times he began to shake, then his legs began to seize up. At best I could only get him to shuffle slowly forward, almost robotic in motion. I managed to get out of him that his tablets were becoming less effective and could we get the hell out of there? This was easier said than done as the mazes are built for fun, which is fine for those of a particular bent in solving puzzles of this nature. Fun was not the word that could be applied to those who panic easily, especially if the exit is nowhere in sight. Luckily a man who had made it to the top of the tower in the maze centre saw my predicament and rushed to our aid. I took George the ten miles back to the care home, and with the aid of one of the workers we extracted, which is the best way to describe the only successful action we took, him from the car. George was still happy to come out with me after this but needless to say safer forms of entertainment were sought. Due to his being in a care home, funding was limited and we had to withdraw my services in a shorter time than both of us would have liked.

I wouldn't make a similar mistake with Andy. For good measure I was sent on a one-day course with the specialist nurse who had referred him to us.

I first started supporting Andy in the winter and we'd walk into town and spend a happy hour or two in cafes and pubs. He liked to play pool and although I enjoyed the odd game, I soon realised how confused he could become after a while. He would now and again use one of the coloured balls as though it were the white one. I wasn't sure whether to correct him or not but never did, as I felt by doing so games might take longer than the time which he had been allocated, they seemed to go on and on as it was. Had he fancied a game of snooker I would have to have cancelled my next two appointments. As the weather warmed up he wanted to get out into the fresh air, and so we went for walks out in the countryside. This coincided with the muck spreading season which nearly caught us out once, but if a client was willing to risk a splattering of muck from a enthusiastic tractor driver, who was I to gainsay it. He was quite sure-footed although he did lurch a bit at times, but was still happy to try out a spot of hill walking. We sought moderate distance walks that I hadn't been on up till then. These were more or less successful despite my mediocre map reading skills. There were one or two exceptions where we had to crawl under a barbed-wire fence to get onto a footpath that we should have been on in the first place. Another time we were enjoying a scenic walk when we came to a field over which was a legitimate footpath, when I noticed a sign. It read; "In this field resides Phil the bull and a few of his friends". Because the field sloped up to a small wood we couldn't tell whether Phil and his bloody friends were there at all. We decided that if he was in residence, as the sign put it, he may not take too kindly to two weary ramblers, even if we did know him by name. We retraced our steps, slightly annoyed, that a farmer in a cunning sort of way had discouraged folks from walking on his land by putting up a seemingly polite notice. One day I arrived at Andy's house to be confronted by a smiling face with his hands clasping something behind his back. Quick as a flash, a gleaming metal detector appeared before my eyes.

This was a nice surprise, not only because I had an appropriate spade that would do the job but also because up until a few years ago this was one of my hobbies. During my visits to my aunty's farm, although enjoying the days out, I hadn't found anything one could describe as antique.

I thought I struck it lucky one day when I unearthed a bronze belt buckle with a Latin inscription of "Mens Sana In Corpore Sano", which translates as a "healthy mind in a healthy body". With trembling fingers I managed to scrape the dirt away enough to reveal four figures. The first showed a Roman or possibly Greek soldier with a spear in his hand. The second figure appeared to have a round discus-type object in his hand. The third showed another figure who appeared to be thrusting a sword towards an object. Mounting excitement nearly overcame me as I managed to scrape off the dirt from the last figure. It was not hard to imagine my disappointment as a figure holding a cricket bat in his hand was discerned. All might not have been lost but the figure closely resembled a certain Mr Ian Botham. Not that I've got anything against the good man, it's just that it suggested a more modern artefact.

We were fortunate in that our receptionist, who also doubled as bookkeeper and secretary and probably other titles, lived on a farm. Also my elder daughter's father-in-law had a farm in a nearby village, which promised a lot of potential, as part of it was common land. Another larger area was adjacent to a satellite station. This wasn't just any station; it was a satellite earth station, boasting over sixty satellites and was the main operator in broadcasting dramatic worldwide events, including the Falklands War and the fall of the Berlin Wall. One day in particular we were detecting quite close to the wire fence, staring up at the gigantic satellite dishes. As we were getting very few signals, although the wire fence had us going on a couple of occasions, we decided reluctantly to move on to an adjacent field and started again there.

I think I heard it first although there probably wasn't much of an advantage in this, except I was able to stop Andy in waving the metal detector about, as to have done so may have been our downfall. As we looked up a helicopter hovered only a few yards above us, and a man holding what looked like a very unfriendly weapon that even seemed to gleam with evil intent in the sunshine, stared at us with steely eyes. This action threw me at first, perhaps I should have paid more attention to the company's health and safety policy in case there was a chapter informing me what to do in the event of a helicopter attack. My only course of action was to point quickly at the metal detector and mouthed something to the effect that couldn't they see I was a humble support worker, and most definitely not a terrorist. The message seemed to have got through and the military helicopter zoomed away, leaving us both with wide-open mouths. Excitement like this I could have done without but at least Andy didn't seem too bothered by it. On trying the part that constituted the common we spent a fruitless one or more hours in digging up bits of cars and other junk.

As word got around, we were asked to find various lost objects for people. The problem with long-lost objects is that they have a liking to disappear as fast as they can, unless a waiting stone halts their progress. Andy's detector was hardly top of the range; it was a beginner's one, which to my mind was like a double-edged sword. Firstly it meant that we wouldn't have to dig several feet down, only to retrieve a ring pull or a piece of silver cigarette paper, but conversely we were only able to detect objects within a few inches of the ground. My old detector came out of the attic but seemingly it didn't take kindly to being kept in solitary confinement, and rebelled by giving many false signals. It had been an expensive purchase in its day but as with most electronic things, newer ones had come along in leaps and bounds, and even though it was slightly superior to Andy's there wasn't too much in it.

We were still willing to be known as lost relic retrievers, or LRR in my acronym parlance. One day our receptionist asked if we could try and find a valuable ring, which the wife of one of her neighbours had lost many years ago on their front lawn. We weren't given many details, only that the neighbour was a recluse, and now a widower, and we were just to wave at him if he appeared at the doorway. She would however ring him just the same to forewarn him. I wasn't sure about this but we gave it a go. As we started digging, as neatly as we could, I sensed a figure peering from behind one of the house curtains. We moved across the lawn to another area and again noted a slight movement from a different curtain. This particular front garden had had its fair share of visitors in the past by the looks of things, not to mention its fair share of bonfires.

The first house that my wife and I purchased was built in Victorian times. I once dug up an area of approximately two-foot square and two-foot deep. I counted after more time than I cared to remember over forty objects, the vast majority being rusty nails and other junk. The only ray of sunshine was when I unearthed a lead iron. This may sound contradictory but it was a child's toy iron made of lead. It's now displayed on one of the shelves in our conservatory and is now a super-glued lead iron object, having had a few falls from inquisitive hands. I realised that we were up against our objective as far as Clare's neighbour was concerned. Finding anything as small as a ring was like the proverbial needle in a haystack. I shrugged my shoulders in an apologetic gesture at the movement in the curtain; I never did discern a face, as we took our leave. When next I saw Clare she asked if we had gone to her neighbour's house and if we had, had he appeared at the doorway? I described what had happened to which she replied that she was glad we attempted it, and asked if we could search one of her potato fields where one of her workers had lost a priceless necklace. She then, almost as an afterthought, apologised for forgetting to pre-warn her neighbour of our planned visit a few days.

As regards the bracelet, another failure was registered as the field was huge, an entire county could have been fed for many a month with the quantity of potatoes it would have yielded. Also it was so difficult to painstakingly detect across a field trying to ensure that you covered every square foot. During another search however, I was able to locate a gentleman's wrist watch, but that was the extent of our finding valuables for clients; our LRR agency was no more.

For ourselves we found the odd brass weight, fishing weight, pre-decimal coins and other odds and ends that seemed to be of interest to us. However when taken to the local museum they were classed as not very interesting after all. I once pushed an old penny into the soil without Andy looking when we had a blank day. He was delighted to unearth it and what's more the date just happened to match the year of his birth, surprisingly.

I had noticed that Andy was starting to lurch more often and one day whilst walking through a corn field with myself in the lead to pave the way, so to speak, I turned around but he was nowhere to be seen. I retraced my steps and found him lying on his back on the ground. I got him back home safely and made arrangements to see him in two weeks' time, as I was due to be on holiday the following week. When I returned to work I took a telephone call to the effect that Andy had had too many falls and had been put into a care home. I visited him there once but the sad fact dawned on me that there was no suitable homes around. At forty-five years of age he had been allocated a room in an old people's care home, as it was known then. To make matters worse his room was adjacent to the TV room and the *Neighbours* theme tune was clearly heard on my visit.

EiGHT

JOHN

John was referred to us by one of the stroke team. The support money came from two different funds and enabled us to have more freedom than with the vast majority of our clients. The lead-up to his stroke was such that it couldn't really be made up, even by fairy-tale standards. He had been travelling to one of the towns in the north of the county when the stroke took hold. The last thing he remembered was seeing the one and only lay-by on that stretch of road directly ahead. He managed to drive into it before he passed out. The car was probably brought to a halt when he took his foot from the clutch, thus stalling it. At that precise moment an ambulance coming the other way saw that something was amiss, and pulled into the lay-by. Had they not done so, it was estimated he would have been a goner in a very short space of time. God clearly hadn't finished with him yet, but whether he would have approved of our visits to the races was open for debate.

John had a part-time secretary, so dealing with paperwork wasn't necessary from my point of view, but Scrabble certainly was. We had an enjoyable routine and I always looked forward to my Tuesday afternoons with John, especially as the mornings could sometimes be a bit trying.

A man in the city had been referred to us as needing support with his paperwork. He lived in a block of flats but there was an issue with his neighbour and unfortunately they shared a communal wall. Both seemed at fault and would aggravate the other with their individual volume controls. I would tread carefully when visiting lest his neighbour saw me and showed off or suddenly upped the volume. I got on well with Bob but that was before his neighbour was also referred to me. I tried to anticipate when Bob might have gone out when visiting his neighbour, and it worked to a degree as it took a while for him to catch on. However once he saw me at his neighbour's door he decided he didn't really need any more support, although in fairness we had reached the end of what we could do for him. I still felt guilty as I tiptoed past his door, when visiting Alan, his neighbour. I would have to think about investing in a pair of brothel creepers if it continued but fortunately I was able to set up another support agency for Alan before that time. Things could have been worse as a lady who lived in an upstairs flat in the complex decided she would also like to be supported. Luckily one of the lady support workers was free and was able to accommodate this new referral.

It was often a relief to finish with disputing neighbours and to enjoy a more relaxed atmosphere. Initially John struggled with the Scrabble and after notching up a couple of big scores, I eased up on the high-scoring words. For instance where I could have had the word 'foxglove', I would leave off the 'fox'. As the weeks went by John caught up with gusto. It wasn't long before I felt compelled to make whatever words would give me maximum points where I could.

When the steeplechase horse racing season began he expressed a desire to attend if that was okay with me. Although never having been racing before I was more than willing to accompany him as a support worker. The only thing I knew about horse racing was what I had read, in various crime-based books, written by former jockeys, and as such armed with the knowledge of how to spot a horse-related criminal activity, I looked forward to this new venture. As John was a wheelchair user and unable even to stand properly, we had to find a reliable taxi firm which would cater for his powered wheelchair. A friendly driver who turned out to be a godsend was found, he never let us down once. After our third visit to the local races I realised that John always seemed to pick winners in at least two, usually three of the races, and would often have a second placement on at least one of the others. I would deliberately pick horses that he hadn't selected just to be in competition with him, which meant of course that I hardly ever won. The most I could hope for was on a place bet, as I cheered on flagging horses that just managed to pip others into second or third place. I even had a bet on a horse owned by one of my ex-directors, thinking it must owe me something for the years of hurt and frustration from its owner, but to no avail, it was never in the running. I never did spot any horse related criminal activity, although the way his horse limped in, it did make my wonder.

John liked his whiskey and I would happily queue up to bring him his double or two. Perhaps it helped him in picking winners, as it didn't seem to have affected his ability to do so. In the end I put money on some of his horses and at least managed to collect some winnings. He would go home usually with a smile on his face. He had a good relationship with his two daughters, who often popped in, and his ex-wife – whom he said he'd done wrong, although he never expanded on this – often called on a fairly regular basis. He was grateful for his family's company and for their concern, and also to anyone else who happened to visit. Things were going too well, but as often happened, to my disappointment, I was asked to give up John and move on to someone with more complex needs.

It was shortly after this I had a big decision to make. I was finding it increasingly difficult to keep two jobs running. Although I made an early start with the household residents, taking them to their activities, I often arrived late for my service users under the various funding. This was mainly due to the teacher/trainer turning up late, on one occasion not at all. Or perhaps the traffic was more congested than usual and the infuriating feeling of wasting one's time being stuck when there was work to be done materialised frequently. Help came with my other job. My manager at the Supporting People job offered me extra hours, within reason as many as I wanted. This was a no brainer but I did find it difficult handing in my notice to my other job. Also it was just after Christmas, which was still a busy time shift-wise. It didn't help the situation that my boss had given us all a present for all the work which we had put in during the year. Nevertheless I handed my notice in and tried not to think of any guilty, sentimental feelings but still kept the Christmas present, after all it would have been rude not to.

NINE

THE HOARDERS

ANN

Another client was a lady whose hoarding problem was putting her health at risk. I had seen television programmes on hoarding and was intrigued to find out how people came to that predicament. I knew already how big a challenge it would be. By definition hoarders had great difficulty in throwing anything away, it could distress them greatly to do so. Although opinions may differ slightly I held the common belief that something in their past caused them to hold on to things as a sense of comfort and/or security. Perhaps these elements were something missing in their younger lives. I did realise that it was very easy to upset people classed as hoarders as one's sense of what they needed to throw away was not in any way their sense. Arguments could escalate if one wasn't careful.

I was able to take Sue, one of the workers covering that particular area of the county, with me, as from the outset it had all the makings of a two-person support job. We pulled up outside a late Victorian terraced house in a southern town. There were a few indications of a clutter problem, but not too much I noted, as we walked up the short path that led to the front door. I suppose we should have realised what we were up against as it took Ann, the lady in question, several minutes to open it. We entered through a cloud of dust, which had been let loose as Ann pushed away a pile of old clothes to allow us access to the front room. As we entered and introduced ourselves we realised the extent of the problem. Clutter had been piled up to four-foot high in some places, with narrow pathways which snaked around the room we stood in. On the approach into the next room, which I gather was once called a dining room, we observed a bucket under the archway. Ann explained that sometimes it was necessary when she was unable to get to the bathroom in time. The dining room was no different to the front room and this led to the bathroom, still at ground level, but both cluttered to the same extent as the rest of the house.

Our hearts went out to her; once expensive but now moth-eaten curtains at half mast completed the picture of desolation. I doubted whether the sun, when it shone through the lounge window, would have had any warming or cheerful impact. Ann shook her head sadly as she gestured with a sweep of her hand to show the concern she felt. To get the ball rolling, although I had serious doubts if it would have done any good, even if it turned out to be an industrial machine, I asked if she had a shredder in her house. She beamed at me in a hopeful optimistic way as she remembered that she did have one. The problem was she couldn't remember where she had put it. Sue and I set to work looking for the missing shredder. After twenty minutes or so I came across a handle sticking out of a pile of rubble. It was attached to a small plastic collection box, which in itself incorporated a set of metal teeth. I couldn't recall having seen a handle-turning manual shredder before.

I picked it up and before I could say anything Ann exclaimed in a loud voice, "Oh you've found it, well done you." I looked at Sue who was hiding behind a pile of debris and out of Ann's sight, trying desperately not to burst out laughing.

"Is this the only one you have?" I asked.

The reply was a classic; "It is, I'm afraid, you'll just have to take it in turns."

Sue and I decided to break chores down in stages with Ann's agreement. I started with the magazines, while Sue began with the clothes if my memory serves me right. Looking through old copies of *Reader's Digest* and other similar magazines, I sensed Ann was right behind me.

Peering over my shoulder she exclaimed that she had been looking for that particular article; June 1967 was presumably a good month for tips on milking goats. She asked if I would put it somewhere safe. Try as I might I couldn't convince her that magazines such as these were a good start in the act of de-cluttering. These barriers continued, and every object we picked up she wanted to see if it was too sentimental to throw away. I must admit I always assumed that most items in a hoarder's house were at least semi-valuable, if not in monetary terms at least in a sentimental way. I hadn't conceived the notion of piles of magazines and old papers being part of this emotional hanging on to things.

I could sympathise to a certain extent as I liked to collect things myself, but more from the viewpoint that they might come in useful than anything else. It was lucky I had a big shed and I suppose having been in engineering I was interested in all manner of engineered objects. Who, following similar interests, could not take some delight in seeing unusual metal shaped objects and wonder as to their manufacture? Whether it be a cast object, a welded object or even a forged one? My collection of brackets and various knick-knacks came in useful on a couple of occasions. One such type which I could have thrown away a few years previous but didn't, had the exact contour and fit to prop up an indoor aerial in my conservatory. Times like this justified my mini collection, although my other half took some convincing. I kept several nice offcuts of wood and usually found uses for them. Perhaps I tended to value wood because previous occupants of my house seemed to be collectors of woodworm-infested furniture. The miniature squatters lived in several areas of my house. The loft, several skirting boards, and timber joists, not to mention most of the woodwork in the garage, were all indiscriminately targeted. Tiny insects would poke their heads out now and again as if to say "Catch us if you can". I spent many an hour, and not necessarily happy ones, armed with gloves, dust masks and five-gallon tins of woodworm killer. It wasn't made any easier by the fact it had been a hot summer and air conditioning was not an option.

Ann wasn't a big talker but one snippet of information she did divulge, which probably threw light on why she felt the need to hoard, was because she had been born illegitimately in a small village. She said it in a way that came across as a penance. Was this the main reason behind her hoarding, I speculated? How tremendously sad that she had been a butt of disapproval by scandalmongers.

We realised that we weren't going to make much, if any at all, impression on the problem and spoke to her social worker about it. Within a short space of time Ann agreed to move into a care home. We visited her once at the home to see if there was anything we could do. All she wanted was for us to fetch five items from the house. It seemed inconceivable that in all that time of collecting things and not disposing of them, she only wanted the five items. It did however take us two hours to retrieve them.

KEN

Ken wasn't a natural hoarder. He became one by accident. He was another client living with a degenerative disorder of the nervous system, and as with others in this unenviable condition I couldn't always make out everything he said. He was renting a flat through a private landlord but unfortunately was behind on the rent. Also his social worker was concerned that the clutter around him was posing a trip hazard. This was exaggerated because of the leads from sockets to laptops and various other electrical wires that lay across every room. It was as though somebody had devised a maze comprised solely of computers, DVD players and their related electrical leads. The reason behind this strange pattern of electrical goods was his lack of patience in understanding related instructions, discarding computers, DVD players and even the odd television that he bought when they didn't do as he thought they should, he'd go out and buy another model. He might have saved himself a great deal of money had he returned them to the shop or even had he hired someone who knew what they were doing. Because of his obsession other factors were neglected, and we noted a new Audi in his driveway. This was only of concern because he had been medically instructed not to drive. It must have been a desirable Audi at one stage, but unfortunately a large dent in one of the wings made it less so.

Again it was felt that a visit by two of us would make a bigger impression although we could still only touch on the periphery of the problem. The first priority was to sort out his finances. He simply couldn't afford to go on as he was, as there wasn't enough money in the pot. We managed to come to some sort of agreement with the landlord's agent, albeit on a temporary basis. We wrote to the Audi dealers with regard to the car, which was on credit, but amazingly in all the time that we supported him, we heard nothing. I can't remember the exact amount he owed, but the sum involved would have bought three or four Vauxhall Corsas, the car I was presently driving. Between us, we compiled a letter stating that Ken no longer wanted the car. We informed them where they could pick it up from, and where the keys were kept. We then cleared out a large amount of clutter, which included out-of-date food along with kitchen utensils and phone chargers that didn't seem to fit any of the phones he kept.

Ken had a few problems with his teeth and on occasions I'd take him to the dentist. One day I'd left him in the waiting room and went to fetch him a cigarette lighter from my car. As I locked the car shut an alarm went off, not that my Corsa was to blame – it didn't have the luxury of such security aids. I walked back to the dentist but was intrigued as to why the alarm was still ringing loudly in my ears, and why were people staring at me like that? I must admit I had to laugh too, when one of the receptionists pointed to my flashing rape alarm. This was standard issue to all support workers, and worked when the pin was pulled out, inadvertently as in this case or otherwise, but I'd forgotten it was attached to my key ring.

We were in constant communication with Ken's social worker and she was very concerned about his situation. With her help she had allocated a place in a local care home, which he initially rejected, but when he realised he could store the bulk of his goods in a storage facility, he at length agreed. His room was in the older part of a farmhouse and was considerably smaller than those in the newer building located alongside the farmhouse. He could however upgrade at a later date when one of the newer rooms became free. The phrase 'dead man's shoes' came to mind.

We spent a good hour or two watching the van man unload the goods into two huge storage cages. I would have to distract Ken during this time otherwise an extra computer or two would have ended up in his new room. The man with a van had moved him a couple of times and as would happen later in the year, he would have to do the same again. But for the time being Ken was reasonably content in his new room, and the care home's technical support worker had his hands full in sorting out laptops and televisions. I visited on a weekly basis, as it was felt support was still necessary due to the piles of bills and assorted unopened letters. I had a telephone call on a day I wouldn't normally see him. When I made the visit he told me he wanted to leave. He had found it restrictive at the care home, doors were locked to keep some of the residents from wandering and it was necessary to ask a member of staff to let him out. It didn't help that a large dog stood sentinel at the doorway. It wasn't however considered vicious, a testament to people falling on top of it and surviving was proof enough.

The main problem for Ken was his unsteadiness on his feet so he didn't feel up to chancing things. Also the care home was in the country and costing him a fortune in taxis. Ken and his social worker had been in contact with a manager from a retirement scheme, which differed from an average care home in that there was more freedom, bigger rooms and several in-house activities. It was also in the middle of a town, sixteen miles from where he currently resided. Again our man with a van, who was probably getting richer by the months, was contacted, and another move was done.

My first visit to his new residence had me once again stepping over electrical debris to get to him and despite other advantages of being there, there was nobody in the building who could help him in a technical way. Six months later another move brought him back to the city, and he became one of the first residents in a new retirement home. This home had its own support worker and as such I lost contact with him. For several months afterwards I often wondered how his next move went.

BETH

Beth lived with her teenage daughter in a three-bedroom house. The housing company who owned the house had several concerns, not least the fact that every downstairs room was full of clutter, mostly magazines but also toys, clothes and much bric-a-brac. Again we teamed up, as hostile neighbours would delight in name-calling anybody who visited the mother and daughter. The front door opened quite easily, but clutter-wise, that was as far as it went. We were soon met with a mountain of items that looked like a profile of the Rockies. I was tasked to carry out an action plan and looked round for space in which to squat down and take notes. I soon realised there wasn't any. Sarah, who had come with me on the day, thought she found somewhere to sit down but jumped up quickly as a mini avalanche threatened to engulf her. This seemed to be mainly made up of magazines that heavily featured half-clad reality stars. The mother was very defensive about her daughter, as social workers were involved, and she was careful not to say anything out of order. Sarah was more informed about the situation and was able to say the right things, even to the daughter who hid behind her mother, and was understandably concerned that we might have a go at her. The abuse she suffered was apparently more than just bullying by others. Unfortunately we weren't able to make too many inroads to the problem because of the underlying problems with the daughter, the neighbours, and the housing situation in general, and it was eventually taken out of our hands. It also didn't help that on our second visit Beth lit a candle on top of the clutter in order, in her words, to clear the vibrations and purify the atmosphere. It doesn't take much imagination to visualise the speed of two open-mouthed support workers as they exited the house.

BRiAN

Brian was a pleasant enough character who lived alone. He had a care package in place so his personal needs were well looked after. Again he was probably more of an accidental hoarder than anything else in that he collected certain goods on a vast scale, but tempered this with being quite selective. These were mostly in the form of toy vehicles and he took great delight, not to mention an enormous amount of his carer's time, in going into great detail about the workings of different types. There was also clutter in the form of books, magazines and clothes. The problem was intensified as he lived in a one-bed flat that was smaller in space than average. Brian had a strange but colourful wardrobe of clothes, quite possibly reflecting his love of charity shops, which he wore in his flat, but when out and about tended to dress more conservatively. He used a substantially built mobile scooter, the likes of which I had never seen before. It suited him well, as he was able to travel miles to fetch shopping and visit family. There wasn't an awful lot we did for him, as his carers –besides the personal care duties – also helped in other aspects as well. I did manage to negotiate a reduction on his telephone related contract, the benefits of which he never used. I found myself popping in to listen to his technical conversations more often than not, some of which I had my doubts as to their correctness. Still at least I now know why Thunderbird Two can outrun Thunderbird Four, or is it the other way round?

JUNE

June lived alone in social housing on the edge of a village. Her landlords were concerned that her clutter problem constituted a health and fire hazard and her finances and paperwork in general would need looking at. I called at her house one summer's morning and initially things didn't look too bad; there were clothes and odds and sods climbing the stairs and apparently piles of clutter in the bedroom as well, but downstairs it was relatively clear. She was a very pleasant lady in her eighties and was easily taken advantage of by one of her neighbours. June being very kind-hearted used to allow her neighbour to climb on her back in order to go from her downstairs bedroom to the outside toilet, and then back again. She knew it could result in a serious injury but didn't want me to report it or even try and sort it out. As I sat down in her lounge to carry out the usual assessments I noticed two or three books about the infamous Fred West.

"Sorry June," I began, "but I was told you were, well, not to put too find a point on it ,illiterate." She replied that that was correct. "Can I ask why you have got several books on the infamous Fred West?"

"Yes," she replied, "he was a relation of mine so I knew him quite well. At least I can look at the photos in the books."

Whenever she brought up this fact in future she would always add, "It was her, not him was the bad 'un," perhaps forgetting the fact that he'd killed at least one other before he met her. Also whenever I looked out of the window she would often say, "There's no bodies buried in my garden, despite what the police might think, just because he used to visit us sometimes."

In order to maintain regular visits I introduced her to a support worker who best covered her area, and between us we kept up weekly sessions, until the housing officers were reasonably satisfied that the house was as good as it was going to be clutter-wise. I did like June but not always when she rang the office as she used to say to the receptionist, "I'd like to speak to the old man if that's alright."

TEN

GEORGE B

George was in his mid-seventies and an amputee. He suffered from that strange phenomenon where he could still sense his missing leg. His wife had died several years previously but whilst still in a reasonable state of mind, had sold the house they shared, and bought the present home whilst he was still in hospital. He told me he knew nothing about it until the ambulance took him there. At least he now lived in a bungalow, which was more beneficial given his present circumstances. Also it was situated within one hundred yards of a supermarket; this was to come in extremely useful over the months. George lived with his dog, a Patterdale terrier, a friendly enough dog, in fact too friendly for my liking. It had an uncanny knack of sensing whenever I was in the vicinity as it was always there to greet me by wagging its tail. As I sat down on the settee, within seconds I had a face more wet than when I usually washed. This made dealing with George's paperwork a difficult task. When next I saw my co-ordinator I presented her with this difficulty and she suggested taking the dog out walking first before seeing to his agenda. I was also to spend an extra half hour to achieve this. The funding didn't really cover dog walking but we felt we had no alternative. George was all for this and told me of a nice country walk starting within 400 yards of the house.

The first fact I established was with regard to dog accessibility. When I was working at the residents' home, one of the tasks was to walk the live-in Trail-hound. The dog was peaceful enough but had a tendency to notch up a fair few victims by way of tripping them up. It was bought from a dog-related rescue charity but there was something not quite right with the paperwork that came with it. The dog was clearly not the five years old it was meant to be, but it was difficult to say exactly what the disparity in years was. It proved to be what I could only describe as a doggie sludge gulper. Every time I took it for a walk it kept its mouth constantly less than an inch from the road or pavement. Many were the times I extracted plastic items from its mouth. It wasn't that we didn't feed it enough, it was just the animal equivalent of a vacuum cleaner. It wasn't safe for the residents to take the dog lead, as even I could barely hold on as we struggled from street to street, but they did like to accompany me, and were often bemused by my shouts of frustration as the dog completely ignored my commands.

We did go out into the countryside on one occasion at the request of Richard, one of the residents. By then we had a car given to us for excursions and taking residents to their various activities. Trying to get the dog up into the boot of the car proved a problem until one of the residents remembered that there was a ramp in the shed. The four of us and the dog, which although the numbers might have added up was certainly not a Famous Five venture, were enjoying the walk until we came to the first stile. Two of the residents could climb it, two couldn't and this included the dog. I didn't realise how heavy it was until I hauled it up over the stile. One resident who couldn't climb it, but didn't let on until the others were over, suddenly decided he'd had enough of country walking and asked if we could go home. The others agreed, the dog was lifted back over and we returned to the car, albeit in a less energetic state.

George assured me the walk he had in mind was perfectly suitable. The first two walks with Willow were fine; it was a pleasant enough stroll after crossing a couple of roads and walking down a quiet lane. This led into two fields, which later on met up with the lane further up. It helped that I first started supporting George during the springtime. It was on the third time that whilst walking in the middle of a field, with the dog off the lead, a shotgun went off a few hundred yards away. In less than four seconds the dog had disappeared from sight. I dashed across the field but was still unable to see him. Not knowing which way the dog had gone I felt I had no option but to return to George and hoped I wouldn't encounter a dead animal on one of the roads I had to traverse. I wasn't sure how to put it to him, after all it wasn't my fault but I still felt extremely guilty. As I arrived at George's door, there was Willow wagging his tail as though I had just arrived that day.

Although Willow was friendly to me, he did have his moments. Again on our walk, a couple happened to pass by, when Willow despite being on a lead at the time bared his teeth and proceeded to tear a small proportion of the man's trousers. I was amazed at the tenacity and speed of the dog. The man obviously wasn't so impressed, and tried to kick him. I made an apology to the man and informed him that I was just the dog walker, but he wasn't in the mood for my contrition and demanded to know the address of Willow's owner. I gave this with reservations but forewarned George with a mobile phone call. When I returned, the man had indeed knocked on George's door and asked for ten pounds' compensation.

Willow bared his teeth one more time when one of the other support workers was shadowing me. A teenager had come over to talk to us and as we stood discussing things, the dog went for the lad with a vengeance. I managed to pull him back but he still managed to get his teeth around his trousers. The lad walked quickly away and I expected some repercussions, but there were none, not even a demand for ten pounds. I did mouth an apology and he seemed to accept this but I vowed to keep Willow on as short a lead as possible after this. Besides sorting through paperwork, I accompanied George the hundred yards or so to the supermarket. Although he had a prosthetic leg and a walking frame, he had fallen over on more than one occasion and was reluctant to make the walk by himself. The girls all knew him in the supermarket and he was treated almost like royalty. He never wanted much in the way of shopping so we only left his bungalow with a couple of bags, but it was not uncommon to take twenty minutes to walk the hundred yards. However he never fell over once in my company. We took slightly longer walking back as it was uphill, but he maintained that the exercise was doing him good.

One of the chief disability benefits someone can apply for when they reach the age of sixty-five years was the attendance allowance. This benefit was to provide financial support to enable those to better manage their lives. The money involved was hardly life-changing amounts but was designed to help people with such things as paying for taxi fares or having home help. It came in two versions; the lower rate and the higher rate. The lower rate was paid to those who needed help during the day. This could include hiring a cleaner or gardener, assuming you were unable to carry out these functions due to your disabilities. The higher rate was paid to those who might also need support during the night time. It was tax-free and didn't have any affect on any other monies that you were receiving. Sometimes when we started to support people who were paid attendance allowance, but were on the lower rate, we would be asked if we could get them on to the higher rate. As far as I can remember the process, although I may have forgotten one or two issues, involved filling in a convoluted form whereby we had to consider several things. This could include the client having had any falls, any struggles with cooking or maintaining the house, encouragement or reminders by others, and other factors too numerous to mention. Applying for attendance allowance could take a lengthy time as besides the form itself, you were required to supply supporting information such as doctors' letters, care plans and even prescription lists. We always dreaded the "I wonder if you could help me fill in this form" request. I experienced a similar reaction when one of our well intentioned but carefree clients with a 'vice like grip' often asked if he could shake my hand. You knew you had to go through with it, but it was never one of life's more pleasant experiences. In this case you just hoped you were still able to drive home safely. Fortunately George was neither a bone cruncher or someone who was after everything he could get, and was content to continue to receive the lower rate which he was on. Unfortunately I had to give him up and move on to other clients after a while.

ELEVEN

THE QUIET ONES

DANIEL

I took over Daniel from Ellen, another support worker. He had been a wheelchair user for many years and I can't recall the reason behind his condition. Admittedly Ellen did forewarn me that it was a struggle to support him. Not because of any mental issues or even any physical ones he might have. It was mainly because he got bored quickly, as I found out for myself. The thinking behind my taking over was because it was felt that a male worker would do better in supporting him. Perhaps it was hoped I could get him interested in manly pursuits. I shadowed Ellen to gain an introduction, and as I usually do the first time I meet somebody, I observed his surroundings and tried to pick up on a nice picture or other attraction that caught the eye. In Daniel's flat there was nothing that took my fancy and my opening words, which were usually complimentary, were somewhat muted. He did later point out a pair of plastic birds, which were hiding behind a cabinet. I was glad they were well hidden as whenever they detected a movement, they would make one hell of a din, purporting to be chirpy singing birds. It was best they stayed where they were.

The introduction went reasonably well and at least he didn't revert to playing Donkey Kong. There was a couple who lived in the upstairs flat and although they couldn't exactly be described as bullying, they were deemed nuisance neighbours none the less. Daniel had set up a spy camera linked to his television as they often walked around the garden outside his kitchen. They also made a big deal of coming down the stairs into the shared passageway. Whether the noise was intentional or not he wasn't sure, as they weren't the most mobile of people, not to mention the lightest either. The problem I had with this set-up was that it was another distraction. I could sit on his sofa for several minutes trying desperately to find something meaningful to say. I never like long silences, but it wasn't quite as bad as being forgotten altogether. It brought to mind another client who told me that apparently I wasn't everyone's cup of tea, before disappearing into the loo clutching a book. When Daniel wasn't playing on his

Nintendo he was looking into the television to see if his neighbours had surfaced.

I once got him to come with me to a garden centre. I had suggested that if he were to develop even a slight interest in gardening as there was a small patch of land allocated to his flat, albeit in a very limited way, it would get him out of his flat a bit more often. We had to take separate cars, as there was no room for me in his single-seater three-wheeled vehicle. This was obtained through the Motability scheme. This godsend was set up to provide disabled people with a vehicle suitable for their needs. This could be in the form of a powered scooter, saloon car or something more elaborate. I've seen large vehicles, often vans with hydraulic ramps at the back of the vehicle, to enable a powered wheelchair user to gain access to the driver's seat. I've also seen specially adapted controls, which might be in the form of push-button gear changes and hand-operated accelerator buttons. To qualify for this scheme you had to have the higher-rate mobility component on your Disability Living Allowance, which you would cash in for a suitable vehicle. I believe there are other qualifying benefits these days but the three-wheeled Invacar as it was known, which Daniel possessed, was eventually phased out due to safety concerns. Daniel was more than confident in his and had developed a knack of getting by. He would sit on the edge of his driver's seat, collapse his wheelchair, then pick it up, shuffle across and place it by his side. It never failed to impress me how people in wheelchairs managed to get by, by being inventive.

Unfortunately, the "Why don't you try a spot of gardening?" request fell on deaf ears. I couldn't blame him in the least and probably would have done the same myself. As there wasn't really anything we could do for him we came to a mutual decision and withdrew our support.

GEOFF

Geoff was a young man who through playing sport had suffered a head injury. His father had recently passed away and so it was thought that I would at least provide some male company. It was agreed that we meet at a pub halfway between my house and his. He was still able to drive legitimately and I just hoped he knew about drinking responsibly. When I arrived at the rendezvous he was standing at the bar with a pint in his hand. I must admit I hadn't thought what drink I might select, and when Geoff offered to buy me one I felt somewhat obliged to have an alcoholic one and then to return the compliment. This of course wasn't my best moment as at the end of the month when I filled in my expense form, it was pointed out by my manager that I obliviously hadn't read our policy statement. The chapter in question stated quite clearly that consuming alcohol whilst at work was completely forbidden and could result in disciplinary procedures.

Geoff was naturally very quiet and whether because of his injury or perhaps his lack of interest in current affairs we struggled to engage in everyday conversation. We would stand at the bar, as he never liked sitting at tables, resulting at times in a lull as the barmaid pulled pints a few feet away from us. I could see her looking out of the corner of her eye, and wondering whether we had fallen out or not. It didn't help that he tended to mumble quite a bit and often turned his head away from me whilst talking. Again the barmaid thought it quite strange as I peered round the side of his head in an attempt to lip-read him. I had varying degrees of success with this technique, some clients spoke so fast that it was difficult to follow what was being said, let alone try to lip-read them. Others I could make out the gist of their conversations if not the whole. I was however fairly confident, when watching football matches on TV, that I could always lip-read the footballers when they missed an open goal.

Another mumbler I supported who also spoke in a Scouse accent, I found very trying, as there is only so many times you can ask someone to repeat themselves. I did find myself having to make educated guesses on occasions as to his meaning, but sometimes the look of horror on his face when I laughed instead of showing concern about a sad event, made me realise I had guessed wrong.

I did hit on a semi-solution as regards to starting a new topic, with the knowledge that Geoff was from a farming background. I read up and even consulted my brother who was a farmer about certain farming-related topics that might help. Armed with some knowledge about which breed of bulls were the most dangerous, I broached the subject. He took me up on it at once. It seems that in general the dairy bulls are more dangerous than those from beef cattle, made especially more dangerous when people walked in the space between the bull and any cows. My negative experience with bulls happened many years ago, as a schoolboy. I remember crossing a field with fishing rod in hand one Sunday afternoon. I was with a friend who pointed to a reddy-brown coloured bull, probably a Hereford, that was taking notice of us. I dismissed it as curiosity on its part. My friend was at the time carrying an even longer fishing rod than mine, his thinking being it would give him an advantage over me with regard to size of fish, decided to up the pace just in case. We were probably only twenty yards from a stile when it charged us. It was more than one hundred yards away at this point. My friend gave a startled cry before taking off. I followed almost immediately but within seconds it had halved the distance. I just made it over the stile but my fishing rod didn't. The bull stood the other side of the stile for quite some time daring me to retrieve my rod, before it bounded away. It took a while, not to mention a fair degree of bravery, to venture back over the stile, and an even longer time to make the long journey home via the roads. No fish were caught that day.

Geoff and I were getting on better following my new knowledge of farming-related matters, however it wasn't to last. When my farming-related conversations came to an end, he found other things to entertain him.

KEITH

Keith was one of life's nice people, the "salt of the earth" as such people used to be described. He lived in a town in the south of the county not far from where he had been brought up over sixty years previously. I didn't mind too much about the silences with Keith, as there were no awkward moments with him. Everything he said came from the heart, and he was always grateful for whatever we did for him. I wasn't his main support worker but often filled in when times were busy. He was a wheelchair user, and had been for several years. His maisonette was at ground level and from his armchair he could look out on a huge expanse of woodland about four miles away. I could tell by speaking to him and by the longing in his eyes how he wished he could once again stroll through pleasant woodland, especially during springtime. He told me once when he was a schoolboy, and lived in a village on the other side of the wood, it had snowed heavily one day during term time. Thinking that there was no way he could get to school by way of the normal road or pavement route, his father had other ideas and announced that Keith was to put on his wellies and follow him. They made their way through five miles of woodland, which quickly turned whiter and whiter with every minute. The snow crept higher and higher until it came up to the top of his wellies. They eventually made their way to their destination. Keith was only there for half an hour or so when the school closed and returning home took way longer than usual.

He was into collecting electrical bits and pieces, such items as transistor-based circuitry to make transistor radios. The memories they held were precious but practically they had no use. The items or circuits could be skipped but where possible he wanted the more complex ones to go to other collectors, but trying to find people of the same ilk who could appreciate such items were hard to find. We carried out the usual paperwork exercise but often Keith asked if he could go out. As he didn't have a powered chair we pushed him in his wheelchair. I can't really say I looked forward to the trip, as he wasn't far off six-foot tall, and a bit gangly. This combination served to upset the centre of gravity. Pushing Keith the half-mile into town was a big effort, and probably wouldn't be allowed these days, but at least it meant I wouldn't need a gym visit for a day or two.

Keith was a bachelor and I once asked him how he had got away with it. He was very thoughtful, shook his head sadly and told me that he had come close to it on one occasion. "There was a lady once," were his words, but then his voice trailed off. How his life might have changed had he plucked up courage, patched up a disagreement or did whatever it would take to achieve what may have been his destiny in life. One's pride or even hesitation in life's journey could mean a left turn at the crossroad where one should have turned right. Keith lived his life honestly without complaint, well into his seventies.

TWELVE

THE STORY TELLERS, STEPH
AND AN EiGHT-FOOT DiTCH

Over the years I met many who could be described as life's tall-story tellers. One gentleman pushed the boundaries as far as these wondrous tales were concerned. I was never sure if he believed his stories or whether he felt in telling them he had something on you. Perhaps it amounted to a degree or two of control as he tried to wind you up, then confuse you, lest you dared point out some of the shortcomings in his life. Was it at all possible, I wondered, during the last war, whilst working in a Kent hay field, for a humble farm worker to bring down a German fighter plane that had swooped down on a crowd of farm hands, by spearing the pilot with a pitchfork, thus saving the day?

But who was I to question these tales and besides which, I was often thoroughly entertained and always intrigued by people's fertile imaginations.

Sometimes, husbands especially, when being entertained under the appropriate funding, would prefer idle banter, and enjoyed relating stories rather than conforming to what their spouses thought they should do. I was all for this, as I dreaded the "What are you like with jigsaws and can you start one with my husband?" question, which would come from a spouse usually at a safe distance as they disappeared outdoors. I've nothing against jigsaw puzzles as such, in fact for many people they would provide a good source of mental stimulation, it's just that I was hopeless with them. I was probably okay with some of the easier 'Peppa Pig' jigsaws but anything else had me scratching my head. In the ones I had a go at, there was always a vast expanse of blue sky, with some clouds thrown in for good measure. This presumably was in the false notion that it would make things easier, which I never found to be so. It was lucky for me that the other workers who although not exactly falling over themselves, did usually see to the jigsaw people.

One story teller would pick up on certain words but didn't always apply them in the right context. I think the word "histrionics" had him baffled as when referring to certain objects he would often begin by saying, "Shall I tell you the histrionics of this particular one?" It was some time later that either someone had put him right or else he had looked up the meaning of the word histrionics. It wasn't mentioned again and the word "history" took its place.

Sometimes when people are referred to us their only negative issue may be loneliness. Without meaning to downplay this condition, as loneliness can be excruciatingly sad and you wished their lives were better, support couldn't really be justified under the funding although we did look at all possible ways we could accommodate such people.

STEPH

Steph was referred to us by her social worker. She was a forty-two-year-old with poor communicative tendencies. The first time I met her she insisted that we meet in a local pub. She wanted to meet in a specific area away from the main hub, but when I arrived she had changed her mind and we located to the bar area. I can't remember meeting in the same place twice running. Steph lived with her mother and although they got on reasonably well, she felt the need to have a flat of her own. Her father had left the marital home within the previous twelve months and her sister had married and moved away. Another older brother lived nearby. She often had secret calls when I was with her, and would wander out of hearing in order to answer. I was never sure if they were from the same caller but she always seem to return with a strange smiley expression on her face, suggestive of someone who knew a naughty secret.

No matter how much one would implore her to reveal it, she was never going to.

She had her name down on the housing list but as she wasn't homeless as such, she wasn't deemed a priority. Her mother wanted me to be more of an advocate, someone to push her case forward and although she didn't say so, someone to keep her out of trouble. We'd visit the housing allocations team on a fairly regular basis where I tried to get the first word in to the officer, as Steph was prone to say something inappropriate, which resulted in a defensive, barbed comment from the other side of the desk. I usually had to explain as to the meaning behind her comments. I tried not to refer to her condition as much as possible. She drove a car and wished to get nearer to the city as her family home was too isolated for her liking but would still consider a country residence. Although, according to Steph, her driving skills may have been very sharp, they were also very aggressive, hence the high number of points on her licence. I tried not to let her drive me anywhere, even though my boss would probably think it a good idea as it would mean less in the way of claiming for mileage expenses.

Out of the blue a flat, which looked on paper more like a bungalow, was offered to her. It was a few miles out but still nearer the city than where her mother lived. We saw the flat/bungalow together. The social housing complex was a strange layout. It was as though a large z-shaped piece of ground tucked away behind a village had been turned into many one-bedroomed terraced dwellings. We had the keys to Steph's flat but the first thing I noticed as we entered were several indentations on the door. Alarm bells rang in my mind, as I suspected someone had tried to kick the door in, not a good sign, but this didn't deter Steph, in fact she thought it quite amusing. Two weeks after moving in I called on her, only to be told that we were going to Worcester that day, and she would be driving. It wasn't until we had travelled six miles that she told me of another motoring offence.

"What if they ban you from driving?" I asked.

She replied that it wouldn't come to that. She'd been told by someone who was supposedly in the know that it would just be two more points on her driving licence but if they slapped a ban on her, she could always plead her vulnerability and inform whoever of her just having moved into the country. I waited forty minutes outside the court before she came out with a look of anger displayed clearly across her face. "The bastards have banned me from driving," were her first words, then "I trust your insurance covers you to drive any car?" As it happened this was the case so I drove back, before she changed her mind.

I hoped she would learn from this, as I did many years previously, although it was in different circumstances, but speeding was still the common thread. There was a fancy dress disco at a venue twelve miles outside of town. I wasn't feeling too good that day but was persuaded by my friends to go along, also it was put to me that it was my turn to drive. We managed to somehow gather together various outfits that were vaguely suggestive of fancy dress costumes and made it to the venue in good time. Because of my feeling under the weather and also being the driver, I didn't participate in the usual round of drinks. The others seemed quite merry and very chatty as we left the venue, but in a short while I would change that. Three of my friends piled into my car and away we went. I was desperate to get back because I would first have to drop the others off, before I could even think about going home. After ten minutes of driving it was pointed out that we hadn't come that way three or four hours previously. Muttering something under my breath I turned the car around. In desperation I put my foot down in an attempt to make up time. Unfortunately I misjudged a sharp bend and the next thing I knew we were upside down in an eight-foot ditch. It took me a little while to come to terms with events, I think it was only seeing my gear stick and wondering why it was suddenly two feet above me, that the situation became clear. A voice shouted "Don't panic" as he shot out of the car in an outfit that was halfway to resembling an army officer. We hadn't been able to find all of the clothes needed to make up a full outfit. This was followed by a man in half a nurse's outfit who managed to clamber out of the ditch, quickly followed by myself and another friend in various semi-unidentifiable outfits. Four people emerging from a ditch at twelve o'clock at night, in very strange attire, most certainly would have scared the wits out of a passing walker. We must have looked like the military wing of the Young Farmers as we spat out grass and a fair dollop of dirt, fortunately there was nobody about. We walked back to the venue, which was still open and cadged a lift home. The Mini Countryman, my first car, was a write-off and proved an expensive mistake but fortunately not a fatal one.

Steph's ban took the shine off her new move and meant she had to rely on lifts with friends, buses or even taxis. It was going to be a long six months. Another incident that resulted in my continuing to be her advocate one day saw us at the local police station. She had been abused both verbally and physically in a city centre park. The suspects were eventually caught but denied the attack. There were no witnesses willing to come forward but Steph, as far as I know, never had any further problems with them. She was unfortunately still prone to mix with others thought to be unsuitable, but she did know her own mind and promised to contact us or her social worker if she got out of her depth. Besides at least she could now cadge lifts into town.

THiRTEEN

LUXURY, PROMOTiON AND SQUALOR

Den had everything to live for. He was a managing director at a firm who manufactured floor tiles, where the business was on the up and up, but his life changed in a matter of hours. Overnight he had a seizure and the next thing he knew he woke up in hospital surrounded by family and nursing staff. Soon after this he was told that he may never walk again. He found it impossible to apply anything constructive to his work and at a relatively young age retired. The one activity that he could achieve with relative ease was by way of gym exercises. We were able to tap into the Supporting People funding, albeit for a limited time-scale, as exercise was considered relevant, especially if there was a glimmer of a chance that he would make a full or partial recovery. We also worked with stroke victims in the same way, encouraging them to take daily walks, by walking with them and as such building up their confidence and strength.

Den wasn't exactly a tall man but for some reason his new wheelchair was very heavy with huge wheels that took an effort to remove. A risk assessment was carried out purely to enable everything to be safely placed into the back of my car. I realised at this point that I should have been more selective in my choice of vehicle. It was lucky at least that the rear seats of my current car could collapse thus enlarging the storage area. A makeshift ramp was acquired with the objective of sliding the chair up into the boot. Initially I was concerned I would run out of time, in just getting the chair in and out of the car. He lived in a barn conversion that had been transformed a few years before his seizure. It was as though he or his wife looked into the future and could foresee his disability, as it was an ideal environment for him with lots of open space. It was luxury itself, one could probably remain isolated for hours in a game of hide and seek. Seeing Den on a weekly visit was one I always looked forward to. For the first few weeks we'd go to the leisure centre where he could use the exercise machines specifically designed to tighten up the upper body parts. After a while Den moved onto the machines designed to strengthen the lower body. As he could transfer from his wheelchair, this helped greatly.

One day after removing the wheels and heaving the chair into the car, I enquired in a matter-of-fact voice "Same again?" his reply wasn't quite what I expected.

"We're not going to the gym today, are we?"

"Aren't we?"

"No, we are going into the woods to photograph the bluebells." I wasn't sure if photographing bluebells was on the Supporting People's list of things to do, but taken off guard I agreed to his request. We pulled up in the car park of a local wood where I unloaded the chair and located the wheels. Out came Den's camera, a fancy-looking digital SLR Canon. It had quite an impressive zoom range, so I thought that I could just park Den at the entrance to the wood and the zoom would do the rest, but this was not quite what he had in mind. I pushed him through tracks that disappeared all too quickly or turned into a mini bog. I did wonder at one point why he wasn't noticing the many bell-shaped perennial herbs we were passing, but it became apparent it was the vast cluster he was after, and unfortunately it wasn't situated on the periphery of the wood. To be fair he would keep asking if I was okay and reassured me it wasn't much further. I probably gave a sigh of relief when we did come across the main crop, at least he was now almost on top of them. Sometimes when we did the gym visit we would do a bit of shopping afterwards. This ensured his wife had more of a break and we could shop bearing in mind Valentine's Days and other special occasions whereby he could surprise his wife.

I could never anticipate what I got asked by clients. One had requested that I take him to a jazz concert. I was up for this, not that it was my favourite type of music, but seeing a live band was always of interest to me. I persuaded my boss, despite a few misgivings on her part, that it would be good for the client's mental health. She did her best to comply with our request and eventually funding was found, just in time before the big event. I have to admit we saw a very professional outfit and even I couldn't help stamping my feet to the music – well, support workers have got to go with the flow now and again.

Another request took me to see a folk singer in a local theatre. I didn't mind that these were evening events, as I felt I could fit them in quite comfortably.

If I finished with a client at about lunchtime and he or she was country-based, I would take the opportunity to find a nice walk, not that I could finish the whole walk but enough to evaluate suitability etc. One such walk took me within eyeshot of a convent. As I peered through the trees I discerned a figure lying on the ground. I couldn't make out as to the sex of the figure but that was obviously irrelevant. I quickly searched for a gap in the hedge and squeezed through into a field that I noted had been planted fairly recently. Treading down the newly planted vegetables I dashed across the field, only to find another hedge between myself and the body. By this time I had my mobile in hand, poised to ring emergency services, but thought I'd better check the condition of the body before ringing. Finding another gap in the hedge and treading down another vegetable crop I made my way to the body, which was lying face down. It took me a while, staring hard at its back before realisation set in; it amazes me still just how lifelike male scarecrows were in those days, and probably still are. Gingerly I made my way back, trying not to stamp on any more plants.

As I admired Den's garden one day I was particularly drawn to a house that appeared derelict within eyeshot of the garden. It belonged to a neighbour and although deserted was still useful for storing goods and initially it proved a good source of income. As I showed interest in the house Den proceeded to tell me the reason it was not for hiring out. A man from the Midlands had approached his neighbour with a view to hiring it. A price was agreed and the man via two lorry loads proceeded to offload all manner of furniture into the house. All went well for a while until one day the police called and during intense interrogation accused the neighbours, in conjunction with the man, of harbouring stolen goods. The man was also being investigated for a homicide. This wasn't quite what they had in mind in the endeavour to branch out in a financial way, but at least the police soon realised their innocence.

The only downside to being a support worker was that you could lose a client like Den because you became more experienced and would be given more complicated cases. Clients such as Den were given to newer support workers assuming they were okay with the moving and handling aspect, and so he went to another.

In 2007, one of the co-ordinators who covered the east and south of the county decided to leave. The position was up for grabs; all we had to do was apply for this post if we were so inclined. I was very inclined as I already had one or two of my interesting people in that area. I applied and managed to get the position of co-ordinator, which I knew only too well would greatly alter my way of working.

I was to be in charge of one male and five female workers, who between them strategically lived and worked in the relevant areas of the county. I knew two of them as they came into the office when I was there having supervision, but the others I had only heard about. In my experience the vast majority of people who were in this line of work were friendly and caring, but as always in a new job I had a few misgivings, not with others but with myself as far as the responsibility was concerned.

My new role was geared more towards supporting the workers. I still needed to retain a couple of clients, as a whole we were short staffed in certain areas, mine being one. I would divide my time between carrying out fortnightly supervisions with my staff, meeting new clients who had been referred to us, writing up action plans and risk assessments, and ensuring that existing clients were happy with the service we provided. I estimated I would probably spend a third of my time in the office, a third with clients and a third with my staff. I shared an office with five other co-ordinators who each looked after different areas of the county. Besides three offices, there lay a vast warehouse that had previously been occupied by a company of gas fitters. As we also operated a charity shop, the storage area was a great asset to house the goods that were donated, usually through house clearances. We had all manner of goods including gym equipment, books, kitchen utensils, even sofas, beds and furniture.

One day whilst marvelling at some of the items I came across a cine camera and a huge array of slides. They were of somebody's wedding, their family days out, their celebrations, a lifetime summed up in pictures. I didn't know the family concerned but through these slides at least they had left their mark in a limited way for those who cared to see them. I wondered if their descendants were still alive and if so why they had allowed these precious memories to be disposed of, as was very likely the case. Other family photos and slides littered the floor from time to time but there was nothing to be done with these once-coveted memorabilia, other than to consign them to the rubbish skip. Most items were given thinking time in the warehouse before being disposed of. I did however notice that a book entitled *How to Photograph the Nude in the Convenience of One's Own Home*, complete with colourful illustrations, didn't hang around for too long.

I was introduced to my new staff whom I took to very quickly. I hoped there wouldn't be as many dead ends in my new area as there were in the rest of the county, which

I seemed to encounter now and again. When one of the BBC programmes wanted to know of secret places in the country, I thought about applying as my sat-nav often took me to many secret places, without any intention on my part.

I was always interested in geography and tried to memorise as many of the villages and towns in the county as I could. This helped when I struggled to sleep at night as I would go through the villages in my mind, starting with A and going in alphabetical order until I fell asleep. If I reached Z I knew I wasn't in for a particularly good night as I would get wound up trying to think of a village starting with that letter. I never did succeed.

CAROL

Carol was a lady in her forties whose life was always in turmoil. In stockinged feet she stood six foot tall; I often wondered why she chose to ride a bike that was meant for a thirteen-year-old, but at least she was able to wobble to her destinations in relatively quick time. She was another who had an on/off relationship with her partner and when we initially took her on she had decided to leave the flat they shared and ended up sofa-sharing with a variety of friends. Unfortunately it wasn't long before she would fall out with them. She was another client we supported whose whereabouts we were never sure of one week to the next. It was a good job mobile phones had been invented, and providing she hadn't left it at a friend's house, at least we were able to meet up at pre-determined places. She was an only child and her father had left the marital home and disappeared, his whereabouts unknown, leaving her mother very distraught. On the occasions when mother and daughter had made the latest argument up and were speaking, I found myself having to listen to two conversations at the same time. The mother would be bemoaning life and could we support her to move into smaller premises, whilst Carol would alternate between her latest feuds and her desire to find accommodation.

It didn't help matters that Carol was on probation for harassing a neighbour when she was with her partner. I accompanied her to the probation office on a few occasions and thought we were making good progress as she almost saw it through. She was only a few weeks away from coming off it when she sent a series of texts that were considered very unfriendly to say the least, to another ex-friend. By now I was quite used to visiting the police station and probation office and was on nodding terms with most of the officers. Everyone we dealt with was more than helpful but I wasn't sure if this was necessarily a good idea all the time as she felt that they were on her side, and the ones who had complained were the real villains. I suppose people were naturally empathetic towards her, but I constantly reminded her that although it was good to have the authorities on her side in a caring way, it was important to bear in mind that she had to take responsibility for her actions.

A new boyfriend had me doubting as to his suitability. He was one of those people who had an opinion on every subject, and Carol was mesmerised by his apparent knowledge. Who was I to put a spoke into the wheel despite my doubts? Also it annoyed me that I couldn't catch him out. Carol felt that she didn't need us anymore, but I kept her on the books as she was still under the probation service. Sure enough a few weeks later I was asked to go round to her mother's. When I arrived Carol was there, pacing the room. Without a word of greeting she asked if I could visit her now ex-boyfriend and bring back the clothes that apparently he had thrown about in a fit of rage. He wouldn't allow her access to his flat and would only allow me in. I tried to recall whether or not I had upset him, but could think of nothing of the sort and as such had no excuse of declining his offer. As I entered the communal garden I couldn't help but notice someone's possessions scattered across the grass. Kitchen implements and assorted objects lay at various angles to a tree stump, as though they had been placed there ceremonially, but for what intention I had no idea. It dawned on me as I rang the bell that Carol's things may not after all be in the flat and those I had just spied had been those that I was meant to pick up. As it happened Carol's possessions were in both places and scooping up the clothes in the flat under a watchful eye, I then gathered those I felt were more valuable around the tree stump. She would have to pick the bike up at a later point. Besides visiting the council's housing department I spent many weeks in trying to get Carol to focus on non-destructive thoughts, which involved trying to visit places where she wouldn't meet any ex-acquaintances. This wasn't always easy and she was more or less confined to temporarily sleeping at her mother's two-bedroomed house and the less time she spent there the better.

One area of frustration I encountered from time and time was, as in Carol's case, when someone deemed vulnerable but perhaps not bad enough to have any protection, ended up in an unsuitable apartment. The housing department, being desperately short of social housing stock, had in conjunction with social workers, names of private landlords whom when all else failed they could call upon. I suppose she could have considered herself somewhat fortunate when Carol found herself in a dingy apartment in the country. The landlord took umbrage when I referred to it as "a bedsit". It was a good job I didn't include the other word that would have preceded bedsit. He would keep repeating, "Oh you mean her flat." But a room no bigger than the size of a badminton court that served as a bedroom, lounge and kitchen was not in my opinion classed as a flat. I queried the kitchen aspect, but I was told that having running water and a microwave made it so. She shared the bathroom with others in the house who seemed okay in the main, but occasionally some of her goods did go missing. There was no intercom system with which to tell who was calling, not that it would have done much good, as the front door was never kept secure during all the visits I made. When I pointed out my concerns to the housing people they would remind me that when she had been with her partner in their shared flat they had had numerous warnings for unruliness and altercations with neighbours. They were unwilling to take her back, especially now that she had a roof over her head. I attended several meetings with housing officers, social workers and even the police but she was still there two years later when this particular contract ended.

FOURTEEN

FRED & SAM

Fred had been a wheelchair user for many years. He found it difficult to transfer and relied on support for this. He and his wife had parted, and he was left alone in the cottage but relying on a vast army of carers to see to his needs. Another problem that played on his mind was as to his continued tenancy. His mother had died a few years before we began our support. The house had been left jointly between Fred, his brother and his sister but on the understanding that Fred was entitled to live in the country cottage for as long as he could manage, or until he passed away. As far as we could tell it wasn't too much of a problem with his siblings, but there was understandably an element of unease on his part. He got on well with his main support worker and they had a good rapport going. She attended to his paperwork as and when and gently encouraged him when he was having a bad day. His powered chair was just narrow enough to enable progress in the ground floor of his cottage, although lumps taken out of several walls did slightly belie this.

As I was now the co-ordinator in the area, his support worker introduced me to him, and I took the opportunity to carry out an annual assessment. She had told me that he was lucky to be here as he had experienced a near miss the week before. Fred, trying to be as independent as possible and despite living five miles from the nearest town, had decided to travel to it in his powered wheelchair. Unfortunately country pavements aren't always conducive to such journeys and after a few hundred yards a dip in the pavement tipped Fred's chair and subsequently Fred too onto a busy main road. It was believed two vehicles screeched to a halt in time. As he was unable to extract himself from the chair, it took a few people to get him upright and back onto the pavement. I assumed they turned the chair around and pointed him back towards his cottage.

Undaunted, Fred was determined to somehow get into town and to this aim we helped him go down the Motability route. This resulted in what can only be described as an all-singing all-dancing vehicle. His support worker arrived one day to find a brand new van parked outside his home and he had no trouble in proudly showing it off to her. On pushing a button, the back doors opened and a ramp came down. By manoeuvring his chair he mounted the ramp and was able to shoot forward and fix himself in position at the driver's seat. The accelerator, brake and clutch controls were hand operated. It was an amazing technological piece of engineering, but it did seem to have one flaw, which Fred found to his cost one day. After parking up, he manoeuvred his chair backwards along the van as he normally did, but unfortunately he had somehow forgotten, or in fairness it might have been a fault with the controls, to activate the ramp, and he shot out of the van backwards. Gravity being what it is soon had him dumped onto the ground.

Luckily the neighbours who by now were used to seeing an upended Fred, witnessed the incident and knew what to do.

We had to hand Fred to another provider when contracts were renegotiated. Years later during my retirement I happened to walk past his cottage and observed a different frontage, his van was nowhere to be seen either. A postman was walking by and I asked him if Fred was still in his cottage, but he gave the sad answer that he had passed away a year or two previously.

I was still on call as far as fatherly duties were concerned even if three of my children had left home. I got a call from my younger daughter who had left her car unlocked overnight and in the morning found to her cost that three Easter eggs and her sat-nav had disappeared, and what should she do ? I advised against reporting it, as the police probably wouldn't bother to even look into it, and besides which I promised, somewhat tongue in cheek, to look out for the culprit myself. Although trying to spot a large individual who can get from A to B very quickly could inevitably prove, quite time consuming. I did also make the suggestion that she replace the eggs especially if one of them had my name on it.

The only male member of my team decided to swap teams and settled in one that covered the city. I was to get three new workers over the coming months. I would have thought that people would be queuing at the door when they heard about the vacancies. It was difficult to describe how interesting and fulfilling the job was. How was it possible to talk about some of the likely scenarios, many of which we probably hadn't even encountered ourselves, in an advert? The main problem I established was the salary. Unfortunately support workers, carers and even social workers have never been paid what they are worth, and as such, people I knew who would make good support workers elected for other jobs and missed out on some strange eye-opening but fulfilling times.

Sam was the first worker I took on. She had worked with difficult children for several years and wanted a different way of working, but still with vulnerable people. After all of the usual inductions and Sam saying she had read the health and safety policy all the way through, which was no mean feat, I took her to meet her first client. We took two cars as I had to go on to risk assess a new referral. After leaving my client I had to respond to a call of nature and drove round till I found a gateway and a high hedge. I left the car parked and climbed over the gate. As I followed the hedge I heard a rustle from the other side and realised that I wasn't alone in the vicinity. Visions of a farmer holding a shotgun formed in my mind. I decided to carry on and tried to formulate some sort of excuse should the inevitable confrontation come to a head. I hadn't travelled too many more yards when coming to a gap in the hedge; I took the plunge and turned my head to face my stalker. To my amazement I found myself confronted by a very worried looking Sam. Masking a snigger or two she sought to admonish me for not having told her there were no public loos in the village. I thought it best to find another hedgerow. I was all for having close bonding with my staff, but on the flip side I did have standards to maintain.

Meeting her second client was quite an event in itself. We'd gone to meet her at her home. She was a wheelchair user and had been for some time. I was asking her a series of questions in my role of creating an action plan, but her husband kept butting in. He began by holding his hand up as though he was back at school and asking if he could go to the toilet. After a short while he would butt in regardless. His wife was clearly irritated but felt reluctant to say anything. He kept wanting reassurance that we knew what we were doing and had we had moving and handling training? I assured him both Sam and myself had done this. We were very hot on training and the moving and handling courses were a must for all new staff and regular updates were common. We took his wife round the block to demonstrate our ability to safely push her. Her husband kept persistently asking one question in particular. It was along the lines of, suppose she wants to do something that we disapprove of? Or if not disapproving, nevertheless suppose we deemed it unusual, what would we do? I tried to answer as best I could, bearing in mind that she was of sound mind, I did however wonder why the question was being asked.

It was a week later that Sam rang me at the office. She sounded a bit hoarse and when I asked if there were any problems, she responded, "You know the husband talked about Diane doing something unusual?"

I replied I remembered it well enough.

Sam continued, "Well I've just left her in a jeweller's shop, she wants to spend £4,000 on a ring, what shall I do?"

As Diane was of sound mind then who were we to go against her wishes? I stated perhaps a bit too hesitantly.

"I thought that might be the case," Sam replied, then added, "but one thing is for certain, don't expect me to be hanging around when she tells her husband ."

FiFTEEN

THOSE LEFT BEHiND

Another client I called upon to introduce myself was a lady called Sheila. She lived with her son and her husband. She had had a leg amputated and had various problems over the months with infections. Her bed had been brought downstairs as the family decided against having a stairlift fitted, but this obviously confined her to that particular part of the house. Again paperwork was looked at with regard to benefits but her support worker had done a splendid job. Sheila was very reluctant to leave the house despite having a sturdy NHS wheelchair. Her son offered to push her, as did we, and a couple of times we almost succeeded but she changed her mind at the last minute. On one occasion we even got her out of the front door.

This was probably the main plan of action once other matters had settled down and Sarah, her support worker, worked tirelessly on this task. The husband was having health problems and wanted some support. I had just carried out an assessment when he literally passed away overnight. His wife and son were understandably heartbroken and it wasn't much longer before Sheila herself passed away. This left Clive and his cocker spaniel alone in a three-bed council house.

After much interaction with the council and social workers at length, we were able to get him a small flat in the same vicinity. We weren't sure if he was able to cope but over the following months he surprised us with his independent living.

The only fly in the ointment was the cocker spaniel; it jumped up and barked continually during our visits. It had already rendered the one and only place of comfort, a three-seater settee, useless by chewing the seating part until the springs came through. So to support him we had to stand and shout. The dog didn't readily relish being confined to the hall either, but when we did manage to do so, it wasn't that much quieter. Also Clive managed to talk at great speed and what with the dog, I found myself having to constantly repeat my questions – even then there were some conversations that flew over my head. To get a word in myself I had to anticipate when Clive would feel compelled to pause for breath. It was a trick I had picked up over the months and one that always served me well.

With Clive it was often tempting to repeat what I thought he had just told me in case I missed anything.

We wrote notes and events on his calendar, and times of our next visit. Although more or less illiterate, he seemed to make a good stab at understanding meanings even if he couldn't decipher the exact words. He wasn't always at home when we called, I suspected the empty ferrets cage in his small garden had something to do with this, but we were able to tick the "client living independently" box. A few years later we ticked the "client gets married, after having agreed to give up his ferrets, and lives happily ever after" box.

iAN

I received a call in the office one day, from a Macmillan nurse who had just left a grieving man alone in a five-bedroom manor house. His mother had just died and Ian, the son, was struggling both emotionally and practically. Could we visit as soon as possible was the request. Two of us set off soon after. I forgot to take my sat-nav that day and Ian must have wondered where the hell we were, but eventually we pulled up in a wide driveway, he heard us coming and opened the door for us. After introductions he was keen to tell us that as a family they were by no means destitute, there was money in the way of bonds or something, but when asked where his mother had kept her paperwork he took us to a sideboard. Despite turning over many *Woman's Own* magazines, pamphlets and advertising flyers, very little on the financial side came to light.

As this threatened to be a long search I allocated another support worker who lived the nearest to Ian, in order to provide more support. It would be a considerable amount of time before things would settle down. Over the months she managed to track down evidence of bonds, shares and other financial deals that his mother, and probably his father too, who had died some years previously, had invested in. The problem was that the paperwork was spread all over the house, in cupboards, wardrobes and other hiding places too. There didn't appear to be any will and because of the complexity we had to call in a local solicitor. Ian had two more support workers over the years including myself when the funding stopped.

One serious problem we encountered was Ian's vulnerability when it came to cold callers. We arrived one day to discover a £3,000 organ in his house. To be fair it was the start of a new hobby, but we shuddered as to the money involved. We did offer to look into it but he seemed happy with events. As strange as it sounds one of his support workers used to bring him tractor magazines, donated by another client, but stopped short of bringing up-to-date issues. This was because he would look at the new offers and ask her what she thought of them and should he invest in a new tractor, not that he had ever owned one. At least with magazines a year or so old, all of the offers would be gone.

When we first met Ian he was able to drive, but as his health deteriorated he was unable to do so, so he relied on one of the girls to take him shopping. Because of mobility issues he decided to sleep downstairs. He still rattled about in the house but at least we could find him quickly. As time went on, Ian's hair grew long and he seemed disinclined to have it cut. He would pick and wear clothes from a colourful selection, some of which appeared to have originally been worn by his mother, but he never failed to liven up our day whenever we visited. I'm sure others would have envied him in many ways as he adopted a sort of Bohemian lifestyle, with seemingly very few cares in the world. I for one, always looked forward to my occasional meetings with him. His main support worker looked after him as best she could and took him shopping regularly but his health went downhill fast. Despite being the same age as myself, he ended his days in a nursing home. Ian was persuaded to leave a will, and as he had very few visits from relatives, the money went to a well-known animal charity.

SIXTEEN

ALICE

I was asked to take over a telephone call that one of the other co-ordinators had taken. She realised that the lady caller was in my area but it had taken a good fifteen minutes and five attempts before she could transfer the call. I should have known what I was in for. The caller introduced herself as Alice then began relating her concerns. The butt of her displeasure was with her partner, who had decided he had had enough. He wished to have a separation and sell the cottage which they held in joint names. Without pausing for breath she suddenly announced, "I'm thinking of asking my mother to move in, that'll hold up his proceedings." There was only one problem, I established later; she didn't get on with her mother. Also the fact that her mother didn't want to move seemed to have gone unnoticed by Alice. It was felt that we were able to offer support to both Alice and her mother should the latter request it. I didn't dare ask about the partner in case he was after support as well.

The first time I visited Alice she related one unsettling fact after another, but was intelligent enough to realise that her time at the cottage was limited. I tried to take a few notes to compile an action plan whilst trying to push her sheepdog down, as it was becoming amorous with my leg. It was a good job I wasn't wearing shorts. I wasn't sure how we could help but selected one of the support team who not only lived closest to her, but seemed to have an abundance of patience with clients. The second time I called by to get an update, her partner walked in soon after. He'd moved out some weeks before but would pop in now and again as and when. He was holding a hair dryer and something else I couldn't quite make out. Alice immediately got on the defensive as he began his tirade. It was to the effect that unless she gave him his suit, which she was hiding, he wouldn't give her back her hair dryer. She responded that he could keep the hair dryer but where was her coffee peculator? This went on for a good few minutes with different electrical items being thrown into the mix. Nothing was handed over but I now had some idea as to their domestic assets.

I was getting the hang of writing up risk assessments but this one was testing my ability to come up with something. I did however refer to the sheepdog, and not yet having an inclination as to whether it swung both ways or not, I probably advised all support workers to be on their guard, and suggested that female workers especially should scale down on their smellies. I even suggested there was a small risk of flying plates when parties came together but thankfully I never encountered this eventuality.

The cottage Alice lived in was a picture-postcard country retreat, whereby two cottages had been knocked into one creating several nooks and crannies. A beautiful flower garden had been created and an extensive meadow bordered the whole. The partner had hired a solicitor and was determined to get the cottage on the market; meanwhile Alice was trying to persuade her mother how beneficial it would be to move in with her. Despite my talking to the mother she elected not to be supported as to do so would somehow put her on the same footing as her daughter. I did call one day when the two ladies were together. I was pleased that one of them had made the other a cup of tea, but that appeared to be the extent of their cordiality. As with two people who couldn't see each other's point of view it didn't take much for one to set the other off. They had learnt by now that when the atmosphere got too tense then they would both back down and silence would ensue. It was in these strange surroundings that I found them that day. I did manage to get some sort of conversation going but it was never easy. Eventually Alice had to admit defeat; we even accompanied her to a court session, but the order had gone against her. Another avenue we tried was to arrange for her to have a mental health assessment in the hope that the judge would allow her to stay on medical grounds, but to no avail. The house was put up for sale and probably against her better judgement Alice moved in with her mother.

It wasn't long before we continued our support when Alice had enough of being told what to do and looked to move out. The cottage had been sold and her share of the money came through. The first house I looked at with her was coincidently not far from one I lived in as a child. I distinctly remember the elderly couple who lived there. My mother used to get upset because the husband wouldn't buy his wife, who was a wheelchair user, a television set. He may have had a point in that, in his words, there was nothing but a load of rubbish on the two or three channels that we had in those days, but it probably didn't justify his actions. I recommended the house to Alice but areas have a habit of changing over the years and I'm sure I couldn't recollect the sheer amount of lorries that rumbled by. Many years ago I had willed traffic to pass by, owing in part to one of my more peaceful hobbies, but writing down vehicle registration numbers was never going to endow me with too much street cred. The house was given a "maybe" possibility but I wasn't too optimistic. Numerous other houses were looked at, but nothing could compare with the beautiful cottage she had had to vacate. The best she could do was purchase a semi on the edge of town. As we helped her pack her things prior to moving, I wasn't absolutely sure but there was an item of clothing carefully packed away that looked suspiciously like a man's grey suit.

I gave an interview to a lady who applied for the vacancy supporting those in the east of the region. She was well experienced working with vulnerable people and came across extremely well at the interview and I knew instantly she would fit into the team. This wasn't always the case with workers I took on, as a small percentage for various reasons decided it wasn't for them. However I was fairly convinced this lady would stick to it; I was beginning to get a feeling for these things. As an initiation I took her to visit a new referral I had received which sounded an ideal introduction, but things were never going to be that easy. It involved an elderly couple in the east of the county with a view to sitting with the husband whilst the wife took a well-deserved break. He had been diagnosed some time ago with memory disorders which seemed to intensify at an alarming rate, and result in his following her around the house. The support could be achieved under the carers' short break funding. If it worked out the new lady would be the support worker. We sat down with the client in a lovely detached house overlooking the countryside. We made the usual small talk and the usual enquiries about what to do if so and so should happen. When the wife was satisfied that we were the real thing and could be trusted, she left us to it. We both seemed to hit it off with Derek who smiled quite extensively in our company. We were very patient with him and we were very pleased that things had worked out well.

I had gone back to the office later that afternoon. Derek's wife had wanted to speak to me; I took the call assuming things were still okay. I'd had a few compliments since being promoted but always tried to receive them with a fair degree of modesty, putting my humble "oh thank you" voice on, when answering calls. However on this occasion I hadn't been expecting the tirade down the phone. Why had we been so cruel to Derek? Why had we laughed in his face and why had we teased him about taking his time in the toilet? To say I was taken by surprise would be an understatement, and when someone is verbally attacking you in full force, it's difficult to get your version of events in, and the final parting shot of "What have you got to say to that?" left me speechless before the phone went dead. I was left with a feeling of frustration as I wasn't able to say anything to that, whatever that was. A few weeks later social care rang me, as they had set up the referral and again became quite verbal with regard to the situation. At least I was able to point out the obvious that he would say and do anything to prevent his wife leaving the house. I did feel for the wife and perhaps understandably, we never heard from her again.

SEVENTEEN

PARTNERS STRUGGLING TO COPE

JILL & GEOFFREY

Another urgent referral was for a couple in the south of the county. Jill the wife was a very frail lady who needed assistance to shop and to ensure she wasn't behind with any payments. She found it difficult to walk without her walking frame, which naturally hindered any type of shopping. Her husband Geoffrey had severe memory loss, which made the domestic situation sometimes unbearable and their only child, a son, lived a long way away. I took a support worker who lived near to the couple with me, for the initial meeting. We weren't sure at first whether we were going to be much use as Jill was very quiet and had to think carefully about my questions, whilst Geoffrey would keep saying, "Thank you very much for coming, but we can manage."

Initially there was no response from his wife, and a few silences passed before he would once again pipe up with "I told you both to go, we can manage for ourselves."

It was as though he hadn't spoken as we both looked at his wife. Eventually ignoring her husband completely she asked when we could start, and who was going to sit with Geoffrey whilst she was shopping? So began a weekly shopping and husband-minding session. I thought it only fair that I should sit with Geoffrey rather than one of the team as I could see a struggle in keeping him occupied.

The first week I was unable to make inroads into his interests. I understood that during his working days he had been a bank manager, as indeed my father had been, but when I asked him which bank he worked for, he was unable to tell me. I did hit on a plan when I saw a Scrabble game in one of his cupboards. He seemed quite enthusiastic towards this idea, and for us both it was to occupy a good hour or two. I didn't mind that he made up his own words and more than often ended up the winner. I did once ask him what the word "oxcraze" meant, he couldn't tell me exactly but he was sure he had heard it from somewhere. I did think to ask if he possessed a dictionary but decided it would probably be more fun, to keep to Geoffrey's imaginative vocabulary.

One day his wife was fumbling with her key safe and in a light-hearted moment I ventured a code number, which greatly surprised her. I had known the year of her birth and as with so many older people who thought this would be the best set of numbers for them to remember, it could be fraught with danger. I pointed out the obvious to Jill that other people who may not be so nice, might also work out someone's key safe number, so with her permission I changed the code.

I had once been out with a client and on returning he had forgotten his key safe number. I tried the year of his birth but that didn't work. I asked the year that his sister was born. He asked me why I wanted to know that. I replied he might have used that year as the code, but that didn't work either. I cursed the fact that I hadn't written down the numbers, and rang the office but they had no knowledge of the code either. Taking my coat off I resigned myself to spending a lot more time than I anticipated with the client. I think I was there for a further ninety minutes, going numerically through multiple combinations before the key safe yielded to the correct code. On another occasion a client had moved into a house but only one front door key had been forthcoming. It was felt that if there was a spare, it would probably be locked up in the key safe. Her surprise was evident, as after asking how old she thought the seller was, I produced the spare key within seconds.

Jill carried on shopping with her support worker for a few months until the former became ill and hospitalised, and Geoffrey ended up in a care home.

A story that I heard about around this time involved a granddaughter whose grandmother had just started to live with the onset of dementia. Although able to get around, the grandmother, in an endeavour to maximise the safety aspect, was given a mobile phone and told to ring a member of the family should she find herself in a place she didn't recognise. Sure enough one afternoon a telephone call to the granddaughter came through, and the conversation began, "I think I'm lost."

"Do you know approximately where you are?"

"No."

"Are you in a shop?"

"I think so."

"What sort of goods can you see?"

"Not sure, I don't recognise much at all, but I do know the name of one of the ladies. I think she said either her name or perhaps somebody else's, was Ann Summers."

VERA

Vera was a hoot. She had an ongoing decline in brain function but strangely was able to get about around the village that she lived in without getting lost. Just in case however, she was traceable through the Buddy System. I hadn't heard of it before but as I understood it, you could be paired with another, in this case it was a member of her family and they could tell where she was in the event of an emergency. Her prospective support worker and I met up at Vera's house. She lived with her husband and daughter, and during the action plan and risk assessment she kept coming up with random comments. She would turn to me and say, "You look like a nice man but what's really your game?"

We looked at the funding for the carers' short break as Sasha, her support worker, was happy to take her out, albeit with a few reservations. Although the local cafe were very tolerant of her, Vera could say impromptu comments to other customers. One lady who was looking forward to a nice cream cake was said to have reddened profusely on hearing the comment "Are you sure you should be eating that? Look at the size of you."

People with similar conditions generally do tend to prefer an orderly daily routine, and Vera to some extent was no different. But out of routine she didn't hold back at all, as she weaved her way through life in her own little world. She had a habit of listening intently to a television programme and repeating certain phrases. One day she and Sasha were looking round an old church and Vera had just been watching a murder mystery programme, when she pointed to Sasha, menacingly, in front of startled onlookers and shouted, "Murderer, murderer – she's the murderer." other similar scenarios were enacted and we were sad to lose her. She was another victim of funding cuts.

CHARLES

Charles was another client referred to us for the carers' short break funding. He lived in a town house with his wife and she had so much patience with him, even though he proved a real handful. It was hard to imagine the effort and determination she had to keep him occupied, and still maintain a daily routine. Again he was one in his own little world and I can't remember him speaking a sentence, although I may have been wrong about this. The only times I saw him were for the initial assessment/action plan and to cover for his regular support worker when she took time off. The action plan was easy to formulate; keep Charles entertained to give his wife a break. The risk assessment was less so as there were complications. He was a powerfully built man and liked to do his own thing, which might put him and his support worker in danger. He was so determined at times that no coaxing or remonstrating would deter him as a new support worker who had only joined the team a little while back, and I found out.

I thought it best for two of us to cover on the days his regular support worker was off. We took Charles to a local cafe and all went well, as he drank his tea and ate his cake. But when we went to leave, firstly he wouldn't hand over the money that his wife had given him to the proprietors, despite our pleadings, and secondly he found great difficulty in rising from his seat. It took a while for both issues to be resolved and with apologies to the staff we left the cafe. He headed for one of the supermarkets and we followed him round the aisles. He seemed drawn to the shelves displaying the alcohol and would touch a bottle of wine or two before wandering into another aisle.

We probably followed him in this fashion for a good ten minutes or more, which would incidentally help us in our future individual shopping expeditions, as we now knew the whole layout of the place. On this occasion it wasn't a good ending as Charles collapsed to the ground. Staff rushed to him and although I was a trained first-aider, we couldn't get near him, due to concerned staff who all presumably boasted first-aid certificates. As it happened Charles was okay and as he had sunk to his knees rather that keeled over, he had no worrying head injuries. We did however have to ring his wife who took him home that day.

His initial support worker appeared to be the only one capable of taking him out safely. One of the talents that Charles possessed was his ability to play the organ. Although having severe communicative problems it hadn't diminished his ability to play like a maestro.

Ultimately with this horrendous condition, matters never improve and again the contract finished all too soon.

EiGHTEEN

LiFE'S MYSTERiES AND A
DODGY CAR

One day, during my lunch hour, I was looking at books that had been donated in our warehouse. One book that made me take interest was one whereby different people had written tips, mostly to do with household affairs. I was particularly drawn to one that a lady called Barbara Mayes had written. I can't recall exactly what the tip was about but was interested enough to take notice. In the afternoon I was looking through all of the referral forms when I noticed one that mentioned a certain Barbara Mayes. I dismissed the connection, as the name was a common one and must have applied to hundreds if not thousands of people. I visited Barbara the next day in her very tidy and nostalgic cottage and mentioned the book I had been reading. To my astonishment she was indeed the editor of that particular tip, which she had submitted many years ago. As she was also a service user with the Red Cross our support was limited, but it did leave me wondering as to life's little coincidences.

JULIA

Another event that stayed with me was when I visited a middle-aged single lady living in social housing in a village setting. The referral stated that she was very vulnerable and we were to be extremely patient with her. I called at her house one morning to find her a bit confused as to who I was, despite one of us phoning beforehand. Two dogs in the lounge looked completely at odds with one another, one being a German Shepherd and the other one of the smallest dogs I had ever seen, which seemed to avoid the bigger dog as much as possible. Other animals that regularly came and went were caged outside. Even one of the dogs had been replaced by another, I noted on a later occasion. What struck me on our first meeting was that as I entered the house I saw a large white shadowy figure standing behind her, but at the same time seeming to engulf her. It seems odd to say that I didn't take much notice of this phenomenon as it seemed perfectly natural for it to be there. It was only afterwards that I reflected on the incident. Although I couldn't make out any features of this apparition I knew that it was protective of Julia and was showing me just how troubled she was and that she would require a delicate touch with support. However, because of her restlessness it was difficult to keep track of her movements.

On one visit, which was primarily to introduce her to a support worker, knowing that we ran a charity shop, she asked if we could provide her with a second-hand easy chair. I had shown her a photograph, which was to her liking. Our van driver, who besides being a reliable driver also had many other attributes that we could call on, delivered the chair one morning. In the afternoon I had an angry call from Julia; the chair wasn't the one I had shown her, or if it was it had deteriorated greatly in the moving. I couldn't find our van driver's boss but I asked him anyway to travel the forty-mile round trip and replace the chair with another that she might prefer. When the aforementioned boss discovered my part in this, she wasn't too happy and told me so in a very loud voice, which penetrated into neighbouring offices. It seemed my work-related debits were fast catching up with my newly acquired credits, and if I wasn't careful would soon overtake them. One of Julia's main problems was relationship-related, and although we did our best to support her, only she could really resolve this particular problem.

ALEX

Alex was one of my favourite clients and was one of the first I supported under the carers' short break funding. He was born with an abnormal brain disorder that restricted his ability to control his muscles and only one of his arms worked as it should.

This didn't stop him doing things and it was amazing to see him in the swimming pool, he could keep up with moderately fast swimmers, and would probably be able to rescue me should the occasion arise.

Swimming was probably the main activity he enjoyed. Another was meeting up at cafes for meals, where he would relish looking through the menu. As he knew I would cut up his meat for him, there were no limitations as to choice. He was supported under the slow learning umbrella but this didn't stop him from joining in conversations with others and even taking responsibility for many of his actions. I don't think I ever heard him complain or throw a wobbly. He loved visits to the cinema and I would meet him off the bus and ensure he caught the right one back home at the end of the evening. I wasn't sure where he got his reviews from with regard to his film wish list, but to be fair most of them were relatively entertaining although one or two were a bit suspect. I'd love to have known who recommended certain questionable films to him. It was one thing outlining the plot of *Revenge of the Sith* but another trying to explain some of the raunchy dialogue in *Ted*, although some of the action required no explanation on my part.

Another interest that we both shared was walking. There were numerous pleasant trails not too far from his house, and although he lurched a bit when walking, we often went for miles not always meaning to at times, but never with complaint. One afternoon we were walking down the slightly sloping high street of his home town when he stumbled. I was walking slightly behind him and saw him take off, pitch forward through the air, perform a perfect somersault, as though to a captive audience, then land back on his two feet. I looked round but couldn't find anybody else who seemed to have noticed. I asked if he was okay and he asked why I was asking. When I related this story to others I got the "probably been too long in the sun" look, but I had to know if it was possible even for an athlete to have achieved this, nobody could tell me for sure, but another person I related this story to had witnessed a similar event.

JENNY

Jenny had been one of the 1960s party people. She had mixed with pop stars and other trendy types but now in her sixties, had retired from the high life and had settled into a flat in a West Country town.

Jenny liked to wander endlessly around town. Whether this was because of boredom or some deep-seated mental anguish we weren't really sure. She had been on the books for a few years and when the annual assessment was due, I met up with her and Kelly, her support worker. I was advised not to sit down in the flat as the hygiene wasn't quite up to standard, a fact that my predecessor had already noted and recorded. Jenny did think it a bit odd my standing up, despite her invitation for me to sit on her easy chair whilst carrying out an annual assessment. It was the second time I had cause to visit, again with Kelly, that something amiss occurred. The flat was in a complex and could only be entered by one of the tenants letting us in via an intercom system. Eventually Jenny answered and let us in. We walked along a wide passageway, then turned a corner and I already had my fist raised in order to rap on her door, when to our amazement there was no door to rap, least ways not where it should have been. As we walked in, the very heavy fire door was lying across her lounge floor. Jenny just pointed to it and said she didn't know had it had happened as all she did was push it a bit harder than usual. She kept no tools with which to have caused this, and besides on further inspection the door hinges had been ripped from the door frame, which showed no sign of deterioration. Nobody, not even the carpenters, could understand how a ten-stone, five-foot nine-inch lady had done so much damage. I just hoped she would never take issue with one of us.

JAMES

This was a strange case. I had a call from one of the organisations that referred people to us. The telephone call went along the lines of, "Can you take back a caller called James Ingots?"

I searched our records for his name and replied, "Not really, no."

"Why not?" came the surprised response.

"Because he's dead."

"He can't be, I've only just left him."

"Well according to our records he died six months ago."

"Not withstanding that, could you take him back on anyway? I think your records should have recorded the fact of his moving house, not moving to another dimension."

Sure enough when I went to see him he was indeed alive and kicking. I rang Jane who was his original support worker, she wasn't sure how the mix-up occurred but thought she had heard it from one of the social workers. He was now a wheelchair user and barely left his home. We managed to somehow contact his bank and arrange for one of the support workers to cash a cheque for him. We scrubbed off the word "dead" from his records and substituted it with the word "vulnerable". We covered ourselves as much as possible as handling someone's money is always prone to potential problems. After a while, his personal carers took over which probably suited us better.

DAVID P

I never actually saw David in the flesh, not that I know of least ways. He rang me one day as I sat in the office. He was in a financial mess, was in arrears with the housing department and wanted help with his affairs. He suggested we meet at a well-known coffee shop that afternoon.

As I'd never laid eyes on him before, he gave me a brief description. He was a balding middle-aged man, five-foot eight tall and would probably be wearing a green jacket. I arrived at the appointed time, looked inside the cafe but decided to wait outside. The place was busy at the time, which didn't altogether help my dithering. The first man I asked if he was David gave me a puzzled look and shook his head. Another who seemed to fit the bill was even more adamant in his denial. Two more non-Davids followed, then someone I thought was my man, but unfortunately although happy to talk to me and answering to the name of David, was not the person I came to see. After thirty or so minutes I decided to call it a day before I was reported for loitering. David rang me the next day; where had I been at our appointed hour he wanted to know? He was adamant he'd been in that cafe at the right time. Either I'd missed him completely or perhaps he'd been in the toilet when I peered inside. Other explanations that were suggested to me, somewhat tongue in cheek, were perhaps he was some sort of ghost, or had I considered the fact that he was having me on? As I never heard from him again I had to conclude that the bugger was indeed having me on.

I had always wanted a convertible car and as I was travelling most days, I felt justified in buying one. A Peugeot 207 was for sale several miles away and the small dealer was interested in a part exchange deal. He agreed to bring it to a local car park not far from my home. This he did and after a trial drive we came to a deal, even though he wasn't too keen on my Corsa, but agreed to it in a way that suggested he was doing me a favour. Also it helped his cause in that we were going through a heatwave at the time, and as he kept reiterating, he could sell it the very next day. When the day was set for the exchange I drove to his house and we did the paperwork. After this he gave me one key. I questioned where the other was, as I had been led to believe there was a pair. I was quite obsessive about having two keys as I knew how much it would cost to rescue a car if the one and only key was lost. He stated that the previous owner was his doctor and she had the spare key. As she was thought to be very busy he would approach her at a later time and retrieve the key. Despite this I drove home in a state of euphoria, with the wind in my face. I hadn't thought to buy a peaked cap, as seen in some of the old motor-themed films, I vowed to rectify that at some stage. There were one or two niggling problems I encountered but on ringing the dealer I was assured he would make good at a later date.

The weather was still perfect for open-topped cars and I drove around the county for the next few weeks carrying out assessments, supervision sessions with the girls and sometimes troubleshooting where clients had an issue or two. I tried not to show off too much but at times it may have looked that way. I did come unstuck once or twice as some of the roads in the area were so narrow, and hedgerows and low-lying branches I found had a tendency to want to knock my newly purchased cap from my head.

I was still having a good time despite not hearing from the dealer. Apparently he still hadn't been able to retrieve the spare key, so I decided to write to the doctor and included a self-addressed envelope to enable the key to be sent. She wrote back a week later. There was no spare key, and did I know the car had been a write-off? This wasn't quite the response I was expecting, but I did find it amazing how many times I could fit the words "trading standards" into a couple of sentences, after first making polite conversation with a certain small dealer. Not long after this my money came back. I couldn't believe that he could cheat his own doctor, I hoped for his sake he never had to rely on her for resuscitation. It wasn't quite the end of my topless car craving as I noticed a 307 for sale from a private owner. It was fortunate that my brother-in-law was a mechanic and as I wasn't going to take any chances this time, he had a good look at it for me.

NiNETEEN

RONNiE AND COL

A friend of mine had been privately supporting a gentleman who erred on the eccentric side, or so I was led to believe. He lived alone in a big house and claimed to see strange supernatural apparitions. I thought it a good idea to see how someone in the private sector worked, unfettered at the time by too many rules and regulations. Although the support given was more in the form of practical help, rather than that experienced in the usual role that I was used to, but still intriguing none-the-less. When I made a joint visit to Ronnie's house, my friend had brought his guitar with him, as Ronnie liked to hear acoustic music. In fact he used to fetch an old saucepan or frying pan from the kitchen and beat it with a spoon in time to the song. After my witnessing this spot of camaraderie, Terry my friend took me round the estate. He pointed to an abandoned Volkswagen van sandwiched between two trees. Apparently although owning a large house and estate he didn't have a summer house so had thought a Volkswagen van might be a good substitute. He had wanted the van to be stationed near the French windows that opened onto his lounge but unfortunately he had driven into the side of a tree, which had then skewed the van round, thus trapping it against an adjacent tree. He had jumped out thinking it was as good a spot as any. If he couldn't have the van where he wanted, then so be it, he would give in to circumstances, even if it was fifty yards away from the intended spot.

I looked inside, and was fairly confident in noting that it had never been sat in since coming to rest.

Terry told me of an auction that Ronnie felt compelled to hold. He had decided there were too many household items for one person, so he would sell the most valuable to get some much-needed money. One set of valuable bone china dinner plates were to be auctioned. As the auctioneer stated that there were eight plates to the set, someone pointed out that they could only see seven of them. Terry went in the house to find the missing plate and discovered it in the kitchen sink; Ronnie had only eaten his dinner off it and hadn't thought it might be needed for the auction. When another lot was being auctioned off, Ronnie changed his mind and although the bids were rising steeply, the auctioneer had to stop proceedings, and withdraw the bids as the hapless culprit collected up the dinnerware. The last time I saw Ronnie was on the *Midlands Today* programme when the BBC were interviewing him for his opinion on something or other, I suspected they cut him short as his opinions could go on for some time.

COL

It was a great shame that my younger brother had moved from the area that I was now the co-ordinator for. Col and his wife had moved to a farm in the latter years of the 1990s, which hadn't been occupied since the end of World War Two. The story went that two brothers had been left the farm whilst in their forties but because they had fallen out, they couldn't decide what to do with the farmhouse. They had let the land to neighbouring farmers but the house was left empty. When both in their eighties the brothers seemed to have patched things up, and decided that they'd better do something with the farm as a whole. In stepped my brother and his wife, after I had seen the farm advertised and informed them of it. Whilst the conveyancing was going through they had had to vacate their cottage, and move to a friend's house. I offered to help, this was readily accepted, but when I saw what needed to be done I did question as to the necessity of it all. What did he want with a stuffed fox with a guinea fowl sticking out of its mouth? These were in a glass cage, the whole of which would probably take more than one man to carry. But of course the answer was that he had already sold or discarded everything he didn't want, and everything left was to be transferred. The fox was also a family heirloom, if a dead fox could be considered as one; it had been shot by an ancestor and so was considered priceless.

I hadn't long forgiven Col for spoiling a bonfire night party, even if it was many years ago when he was probably ten or eleven. I was living with my parents at the time and had invited friends to our annual firework display. Half an hour before the main event, Col had kindly, we thought at the time, taken two boxes of fireworks out into the garden. Unknown to us he had also taken out a box of matches and impatience must have got the better of him. *I'll just light the one*, he probably thought and picked up a Roman Candle. Hearing the bang my wife-to-be and I dashed outside as sparks from the Roman Candle decided to maliciously land on the nearest box of fireworks. I came round the corner only to be met by a rocket as it flashed past my eyes. Luckily the door to the summer house was open, we threw ourselves inside and had what can only be described as an unnerving display of loud bangs, and random explosions as rockets and other fast-moving fireworks hit the sides of the houses. When we thought it was all over and got up to remonstrate with my brother, the second box of fireworks decided to join in with the fun. When our friends arrived there was nothing for them to see. I sensed their barely concealed laughter bouts more than made up for the disappointment of being deprived of a free firework display.

The move to the friend's house was made easier as they owned a farm with many outhouses and I found myself poking smallish goods into very dusty corners, in distant recesses and on shelves, just hoping they would be found when the time came to forward them to the new premises. When the paperwork was sorted out everything had to be moved to the new farm, which involved several lorry loads. The farmhouse was in quite a state due to many years of neglect but my brother, as industrious as ever, soon had several rooms made habitable. His DIY manual obviously had less inaccuracies in than mine. The one thing in his favour was at least the two brothers had the foresight to repair the roof when it was seen to be leaking. Over the months the house repairs took place and the animals prospered in the hundred acres or so that came with the farmhouse. My two nephews were born within a relatively short space of time. All seemed to be going well until some neighbours turned against him.

Before Col moved in, one of the barns had fallen down and plans were drawn up to resurrect it. The plans were shown to the neighbours who raised no objection. The problem started when the barn resumed its original shape, and this obscured the view across the valley from some of the neighbours. A retired schoolmaster whom my brother had become friendly with, was asked why the family were being ignored. The neighbour replied that Mrs X had told him not to speak to them. Other incidences followed suit, but when the boys became caught in this web of silence they decided they'd had enough and eventually moved many miles away. Someone had even falsely lied to environmental health about dead sheep lying all over the farm, but inspectors could find no evidence of this. It was yet another indication of saying one is not wanted. It seemed utterly unbelievable that one person could have so much sway over an entire neighbourhood.

TWENTY

SUPERVISIONS, RISK ASSESSMENTS AND ANOTHER GOLFER

I was by now well used to carrying out supervisions, new assessments, action plans and even annual assessments. Risk assessments were sometimes a bit tricky. I probably appeared nosey as I peered into people's front rooms and kitchen areas, in fact anywhere I thought a support worker might have to go. A couple of scenarios had me scratching my head. A lady suffering from dementia opened one of her cupboards only to expose wads of twenty-pound notes. Besides including a warning or two on the risk assessment, I felt compelled to report it to the appropriate people after first pointing out the potential pitfalls to the lady. It was especially important as she had four carer visits daily.

Another similar incident was when a support worker helping clear a house for a lady who was going into a care home came across bags of unopened food. In each bag was the change from the transaction and collectively this amounted to a considerable sum. Often we sent two support workers in where money was concerned and everything was well recorded.

Anything untoward or potentially hazardous was written down. I saw one risk assessment that said "On entering the client's house beware of low flying budgerigars", and indeed when I entered the client's house it was like walking through an aviary.

Another unusual pitfall I discovered was when I drove up a long driveway, which wound its way around sharp bends and was just wide enough for my Peugeot. On getting to the top I found a plateau occupying just enough space to park the car with hardly any room for turning round. I noted the ground sloped away sharply on the three sides, four if you counted the driveway. I was told by the family that it was possible with patience in that a ten point turn was usually necessary, and having a small car helped enormously. As my 307 couldn't transform into this category even though it was a convertible, I had no hesitation in asking one of the family to see me out.

One six-foot man despite his physical difficulties wanted to play a game of snooker. We took him on only by escorting him with two support workers, myself being one of them. As he was a wheelchair user, one of the girls would push him to the table, he would then raise himself up only to face me as his snooker opponent.

We had to make it known to him and his wife that if he fell we would be unable to catch him. It wasn't just his size that prohibited this, had he been a four-foot Hobbit the instruction would still apply, not that I've ever seen a snooker-playing four-foot Hobbit.

A lady we supported for years was unfortunately on the scammers' list. We didn't realise this for quite a while, it was only when she had no money to pay for certain goods that realisation kicked in. Try as we might we were unable to persuade the lady to stop sending money to people who assured her that she would win a million pounds in a so-called lottery, if only she kept up her payments to them. Even her son was unable to dissuade her. Her answer was that it was a sort of hobby, the only one she had, and besides, they promised her she would win "the big one" one day.

The only time the scammers failed to extract money was when she spent months in hospital having broken her hip. Her risk assessment was more of an awareness note as we were powerless to do anything.

One risk assessment was a bit different to say the least but the client, an elderly lady, told me to record it anyway. On noting her birth year on the referral, I couldn't help but exclaim, "I see you were born in 1914, the very year World War One broke out."

She looked at me with a glint in her eye as she responded, "Yes young man, but I want this to be known, I was much too young to start it."

A pre-existing risk assessment on an elderly man suggested that he "likes to wonder". I thought it a bit odd and it made me question as to what sort of wondering was deemed necessary for it to be on a risk assessment. For instance, did he wonder as to who the hell are these people purporting to support me? I had my answer after arranging to see him one day. He wasn't there despite my telephone call just before I set out. When I returned to the office I made sure to change the wording "he likes to wonder" to that of "he likes to wander".

One situation that could have gone disastrously wrong was when I went to a diabetic client's house and after ringing the bell but not getting any answer, I looked through his window and saw him slumped on the floor. I did have the key safe number as this had happened before. Usually he kept bottles of Lucozade in the kitchen, but the ones that were there were all empty, as was the pile of glucose tablets. He was barely conscious as he mouthed the word "Lucozade". I dashed out the house and made my way to the local shop, grabbed two bottles and frustratingly noted the shopkeeper catching up on old times with a customer. Another person was also in the process of queuing. I jumped in front of this startled customer, threw some money on the counter, mouthing the word "emergency" and was back in Adrian's house in no time. The Lucozade brought him round and I remarked how lucky he was. "Not half as lucky as the other day," he replied. "Whilst cutting the grass with my electric mower, I happened to slice through the cable."

It was lucky his electric box had an RCD fitted. The diabetic incident was something to be thought about before calling on him, perhaps a timely phone call to jog his memory of what nearly occurred and to ensure he had a plentiful supply of Lucozade.

Some vulnerable clients were easily led and one man in particular often used to be host to some less desirable friends, whether he wanted to be or not. He was known to social workers not that he posed a threat, but because of his vulnerability others might take advantage of him, although we had no concrete proof of any wrongdoing. The neighbourhood at the time had a spate of drug dealing, although Nick and his friends as far as I could tell kept away from drugs. A man in an upstairs flat was got at by someone who scaled a ladder and was trying to smash the window in. We tried to see Nick in places other than his flat but if this wasn't possible, we would insist on nobody else being there. He did hit on a solution once or twice and we ended up in the silver screen showings at the local cinema, after which I was obliged to see to his paperwork.

His lifestyle was proving a hit and miss affair, but being of sound mind, according to the experts, he was free to choose his own friends and he thought it better to have slightly dodgy friends than none at all.

On a more everyday observation I always searched for wires that constituted trip hazards; amorous dogs; peeling plaster or even slippery paths. This was the cause of one of the support workers' fall one day. She twisted her ankle on a long concrete pathway that had become slippery though rain and mud. It was lucky that she had another worker who was shadowing her, and was able to help her to the car. As we had a relatively small team of workers, they had to cover a large area and we couldn't afford for too many workers to be off. We paid travelling expenses as well as the time spent travelling, albeit both would probably start from the home of the first client of the day, unless they happened to be covering for another in a different area. Sometimes a worker who was stepping in for another might have to travel thirty miles, such was the size of area we covered.

I always looked forward to the fortnightly supervision with the girls, where they could offload problems over a cup of coffee. I think over time, I must have carried out the supervisions in ninety per cent of the cafes in the south and east of the county. This in hindsight was a good idea as seeing five different girls in the same café in the space of five weeks would have set onlookers tongues wagging. Work-wise, life couldn't get much better, but soon events would turn the other way.

DONALD

Donald had been a big player in a well-known engineering group but had experienced a massive setback to his physical health many years before even considering retirement. He lived with his wife in a house on the edge of town and I had inherited him, so to speak, when I took over the area. I didn't have too many volunteers for taking him to play golf but felt I could fit him in as the golf club, besides the impressive eighteen-hole course, also boasted a nine-hole academy one. This was for those not able or not good enough to get round the eighteen holes. As the main course ran parallel to the academy course in sections, I observed some golfers who were struggling, but didn't want to be seen on what they would call the "beginners' course". We were happy to be seen on this lesser course.

I would call at the house, share a piece of cake and a natter, bundle Donald and his clubs into the car and away we would go. On first impressions the course looked tame. The longest hole was a hundred and twenty yards, the shortest one a mere sixty-five yards. The grass was always very neatly cut and there were only a couple of areas where a ball could be lost. There should have been no excuse for lost balls but we were to put this theory to the test.

Holes one and two were a breeze and could easily be accomplished with a number four iron and a putter, but as we progressed through the course the ground rose steeply and hole three was a pig. It was one of the longer holes but with a sloping green. The ball could be hit and land within an inch of the hole, but end up five or six yards from it, depending on how quick you were in putting your foot out to prevent it rolling any further. As we both did it, it didn't seem to matter. The next hole was similar in that it sloped even more steeply if anything, and you had to be even quicker to get your foot in the way. After this we started to go downhill, literally and metaphorically, but at least we could see the finishing line. It was as good a place for us to go to as any, even when it was wet, as then we were able to use the sheltered golf driving range, doing our best to slice balls in the direction of various targets.

During car journeys we often shared amusing sporting stories, which brought back my early cricketing memories. Many years ago I had called at a friend's house as pre-arranged. Unfortunately he had forgotten I was coming and he had arranged to make the six-monthly visit to see his cousin. When I arrived he seemed surprised but pleased to see me and suggested I go with him to his cousin's house. On the bus journey there I asked him why he only made the journey twice a year. "Luke's okay," he began, "but he's cricket mad and always wants me to bowl at him, with you there perhaps we can go exploring or something." He then added, "Whatever you do don't ask him anything about cricket and decline any invitation to play the game."

On arriving at Luke's house he told us to follow him as he had something to show us. We crossed over two fields before he brought us to a third and there laid out in front of us was a cricket pitch complete with a rope, but not enough of it to go completely around, to denote the much-reduced boundary. "Who wants to bat first?" came the inevitable question two of us had dreaded. I looked at my friend but couldn't quite make out his expression as he had his hand firmly pressed to his forehead. As I was the guest so to speak, it was decided I should go first. With a limited number of players one of us batted, one bowled and the other fielded as best they could. I wasn't to last long at the crease. Apparently I was run out, which was a bit difficult to take as there were no visible lines in front of the wicket. My friend didn't last much longer and this brought Luke in. He took his time in patting down the various lumps and bumps, ignored the two cow pats, took guard and rather immodestly, I thought, started to hit the ball for fours. I could sense this being a long session. On the plus side I suppose at least collecting the ball from various areas of the field was a good way of seeing the countryside. I thought I had him LBW on two occasions but apparently you can't be out that way if the ball lands outside the line of leg. Luke being umpire as well as batsman knew all of the rules well enough. It didn't help with any benevolent acts he might have bestowed on us that I inadvertently bowled him a full toss, which caught him on the knee. This didn't go down terribly well, as the only protection he had besides proper batsmen's gloves was one leg guard. Unfortunately for Luke I managed to hit the unprotected knee. Soon after this the fours turned into sixes, but at least the game was over quicker than we anticipated. Luke declared on 101 and we retired for a well-deserved cream tea, before the two of us caught the last bus home.

Many years later I made up the numbers when Moccas my son's cricket club found themselves short. On these occasions I would be put to bat at number eleven but once, (and I do believe they must have made a mistake when writing out the batting order) I was elevated up the dizzy heights to number ten. Even at this elevation I found fast bowlers, usually sixteen year olds who unable to bowl their allotted overs in one go, would be allowed to continue towards the end of the innings. It was never easy, as balls whistled past my head or were aimed cunningly towards other parts of the anatomy I wished to hold onto, of trying to remember the captain's instructions. He would utter the immortal words, " just go out there and enjoy yourself".

I always endeavoured to have supervision in the same area as my client's house, this would save time and lessen my mileage expenses, and with the aid of local maps I planned my workload for the week. By now some of the contracts were coming to an end and the funding for the carers' short break took a big hit.

TWENTY-ONE

JOB TRANSFER (TUPE)

The year 2011 saw some of the council contracts up for grabs. The carers' short break contract had virtually disappeared but the main contract previously called Supporting People was now to be named Housing-Related Support. This contract was much-reduced in value, and would only be awarded to one organisation, instead of several as had been the case up to then, but was still worthwhile in its pursuit. It was the lifeblood of other support agencies, besides ourselves. Various smaller bits of funding wouldn't sustain our organisation. We put in a fair bid and waited and waited. The council had meant for the new providers to start in late 2011 or early 2012 at the latest, but delays meant whoever won the contract wouldn't be able to start until October 2012. We carried on normally taking new clients and carrying out all the needed assessments and supervisions.

Just when we thought we had seen and heard everything, a man was referred to us who had separated from his wife, but still lived in the house that they had bought together. The problem was that it had been condemned, due to various structural issues, and bare electrical wires didn't help the situation either. His wife had left some time before, she wanted the house gone, and to this aim was taking legal advice. Tom, her ex-husband, would sneak round the back of the house and let himself in through the French windows, despite the council's best efforts at boarding up all entry points. I was asked to see what we could do.

"How will I find him?" was the first question to the housing officer.

"He'll probably be in his dining room."

"Yes but if the house is condemned, I won't be allowed in."

"That's right," came the unhelpful reply.

"And?"

"Well with a bit of luck he'll be sleeping in the shed, especially if he can't get into the house."

"Is that condemned too?"

"No, I don't think so."

I wasn't quite sure what to expect on my visit but as I went round the back I saw three figures in his dining room. I did manage to establish which one was Tom and carried out a sort of assessment through the window. He didn't want any support, he just wanted to stay in his house, presumably with his new-found friends. He also had a lady friend who lived in the equivalent of a hostel for women. Being highly skilled at sneaking in to premises unseen, he would often kip down with her. This didn't go down too well with the hostel's governing board but surprisingly they seemed to turn a blind eye at times. There was little we could do for Tom as we never knew where he was, one moment to the next, but we kept him on our books in case he changed his mind. One of the first questions a prospective client asks is how much will it cost them? They couldn't believe that the service was free, although for how much longer we couldn't guarantee.

As decision time got nearer concerns began to mount up, as other organisations we knew of were also in the bidding. Then one day we learnt the truth; the council in their wisdom had given the contract to an organisation outside of the county. The regulation of TUPE came into effect for those wishing to keep their job. TUPE stood for the Transfer Of Undertakings Protection Of Employment and in this case came into effect because another employer had taken the main contract from us. The regulation was brought about to safeguard employees' wages, holiday entitlements and rights in general. We met up with the organisation that had taken our contract. They explained things as to what they could do and gave us the choice of joining them or staying put and taking our chances with our present employer who still tapped into funding, albeit in a limited way. Unfortunately there was no co-ordinator equivalent in the new organisation and I would have to take a pay cut and become a support worker, although I was entitled to a redundancy package. This I agreed to, as at least it would mean another three years of employment. I also negotiated a three-day working week and even spelt out the days I wanted. This was met with their approval, and so began the final chapter of my working life. Seven of our employees also came across. On the day we started our new job we met several others from another organisation who had also lost their share of the contract. The day that it ended one of their managers rounded the workers up, took them to the premises of the new providers and left them outside the door with the parting shot of "Goodbye ex-colleagues". At least we were able to tidy up and say our goodbyes.

The new way of recording facts was different again and we were all issued with laptops and copious instructions on how to use them. Training was first class and we mixed with others from this huge organisation. We were told that we had to do our own action plans and risk assessments, but it was mostly in the form of tick boxes, which was the main difference from our previous way of working. I was okay with this but some of the others were thrown into the fray.

TWENTY-TWO

APPOiNTMENTS

When we were let loose after a week or two I seemed to start off by accompanying people to various appointments.

One concerned a man called Terence, who was one of the first referrals assigned to me. We had an appointment at one of the return-to-work agencies and were to attend a seminar entitled, appropriately enough, "How to get back on the working ladder". Terence clearly didn't want to be there and hardly spoke to the receptionist who tried to make polite conversation. There were three of us who attended the seminar and the lecturer did his best to make things interesting, however the third person, whether by design or otherwise, started asking questions that had no relevance to the seminar. He appeared to be on a bit of an ego trip and tried to make the odd joke. Terence had turned his back on the lecturer with the obvious intention of stating how bored he was. For politeness' sake I feigned interest. That was it; for the rest of the talk I appeared to be a captive audience, he never looked at the other two once. At least I knew what to do should redundancy strike again.

One of the worst types of meetings was where an eviction was involved. A large local estate had been quite happy to take a couple's rent for the last fifteen years but when the couple fell upon hard times they were threatened with eviction. The main issue brought up at the meeting I attended was that the couple had insisted on renting a large farmhouse with many outbuildings, but declined to downsize and take the offer of a smaller house. The added problem was that the husband had been diagnosed with a form of dementia and was totally reliant on local agencies. The estate was apologetic but said they had their hands tied, as the couple were already behind with their rent and were not in a position to catch up.

It was pitiful to see the couple pack their belongings, their mementos of happier times; I wondered whether they had anywhere to store them. I did broach the subject but they appeared to be in a state of denial and felt sure a rescue package at the eleventh hour would be forthcoming. We did manage to make contingency plans whereby the wife would stay with a friend whilst the husband would go into a care home. This plan was put into operation when the miracle failed to materialise. I visited the husband when I felt he had settled down, he seemed okay with the situation but I did note a sense of sadness. One surprising fact that emerged was the rent money they had paid over the years would have bought a nice semi-detached house in the area.

Over the following months my eyes were opened to the fullest extent as I supported clients at probation meetings, court cases, police stations where I was the appropriate adult and other various meetings with professionals.

Sometimes when needs must, we had to act fast. An elderly man who had spent many months in a local hospital was due to be transferred to a care home but needed an advocate to supervise the move. In fact I was asked to visit the care home alone and assess its suitability, then recommend it or otherwise to him on my return. He had lived alone and wasn't in the best of health physically and to a lesser extent mentally, but was deemed well enough to move out. I was to meet up with the gentleman and his social worker, but action was needed quickly as there were no places available at the time, except one vacancy in a home sixteen miles away. I travelled to the hospital and met Eric on my own. I told him about the proposal and promised to take some photos of the intended destination. He was fine with this, then surprised me with "I'm used to change, when you've been on the beaches at Dunkirk waiting to be rescued from the Germans, anything after that is a bonus."

He had never been married and in coming back after the war, lived with his parents and continued his pre-war work as a postman. I set off on a fine spring day but getting to the right place in the care home probably took as long as the journey, as it was a big rambling old house with several extensions. I did note however the beautiful views over the Wye Valley. The home met with my approval, which furthered my recommendation in that a lady independent of the home visited on a weekly basis and arranged outings or other events for the residents. I returned to Eric with my digital camera, showed him photographs and gave him a description as best I could of the general state of the home. He seemed overwhelmed by my enthusiasm and readily agreed to relocate. His social worker took care of the moving arrangements.

When next I called on Eric at the home, one of the care staff nabbed me before I reached his room. She told me he didn't understand the Do Not Resuscitate policy they had in place and could I have a word. Probably the best way of explaining it was to liken it to being on the beaches of Dunkirk, I surmised, not that there was a direct comparison or so I hoped, but he must have seen wounded soldiers being attended to. After mentioning this I asked if he were to experience a life-threatening situation, would he too like to be attended to? Or to phrase it differently, would it be okay with him to receive whatever treatment was necessary to save him. "Oh yes," was his hesitant slightly bewildered reply. The staff member looked at me with a puzzled frown.

"I'm not sure he understood that," she reflected. "And as such I don't know whether to put that down on his records. I just hope you haven't confused him and he's not going to associate us with the German army. Still I suppose it's the best we've got under the circumstances."

I smiled as I walked away, and fervently hoped that for what he had done for the country, in his final few years he would find peace and perhaps some happiness.

TWENTY-THREE

MORE THINKING REQUIRED

MARTIN

My area with the new providers was mostly, but not exclusively, within the city. And one such client named Martin who lived on his own in a three-bed house was referred to us by one of the city's social workers. He had been diagnosed with severe memory loss, and as care workers found it difficult to work with him, a haphazard care arrangement was ongoing. The housing department had him down for a room in a refurbished retirement home not far from where he was living, and through his social worker asked us to pave the way for his relocation. Although he had agreed to the move in theory, when I saw him for the first time he denied having anything to do with it. We had to continually remind him that he couldn't live the way he had been. For one thing the hygiene in the upstairs rooms especially was worrying, and clutter also became an issue. I noted that his next of kin was his brother, and in my most friendly telephone voice I asked if he would help out. The desired answer wasn't forthcoming as he replied, "You don't know him like I do," and put the phone down on me.

Knowing that Martin could take his most treasured belongings with him probably helped the situation. He hung onto this promise even if he was to forget other things that we told him. Possessions from a three-bed house don't always fit readily into a one-bed flat, even if it was on the larger side. One day he agreed to donate some of his large collection of vinyl records, then next day he wanted to keep them all. It was fortunate that he got on well with his next-door neighbour, and she was able to guide Martin as to what she thought would be useful to him in the new place, but we still had a long way to go. The van man that we had used on other occasions was hired, but had his work cut out, as he couldn't take surplus items to charity shops or even to the tip without first asking me if it was okay. I then had to put the question to Martin, whose answer was never predictable.

We also had a deadline; the housing people wanted him out, leaving behind a tidy house. I told them that I couldn't guarantee this, as it seemed that the more we shifted, the more we uncovered other goods. In the end we moved Martin to his new place but had to admit defeat in clearing the house. I don't think I fibbed too much with regard to the extent of the problem, whilst talking to the housing officer on the phone, but I may have omitted to tell him about the heavy cumbersome exercise machines still in his bedroom.

KEN R

Ken was one of those people who expected manual work to be done at minimal cost. He was a pleasant enough man, recently retired, but found it difficult to come to terms with modern ways including monetary inflation. An elderly neighbour who used to do his gardening at pocket-money prices was unable to continue due to a serious health condition. Ken was reluctant to get over this, was indignant and considered such an act was against any human convention. The hard-done-by feeling intensified when the first few quotes he received for the "basic upkeep" as he put it, of his spacious garden, had him tearing his hair out. "They want as much as twenty pounds an hour," he exploded. I tried to set out an argument based on contractors' accountants' fees, insurance premiums, overheads and other sundry expenses but to no avail. He considered all contractors as rip-off merchants. My boss was all for withdrawing our support unless there were other important issues. Armed with her blessing I tried numerous times to end our support, citing others on the waiting list who were desperate to take advantage of the limited resources we were able to offer, and badly needed our support but it fell on deaf ears. He seemed to amass handfuls of paperwork, the bulk of which being invoices on which he wanted a second opinion. Many of these invoices were several months old and I must have looked at the same invoice on numerous occasions, but as he pointed out we were meant to be the paperwork experts.

Although retired himself his wife was still of working age and I never actually met her. Ken informed me that along with himself she wasn't able to manage the gardening either due to similar bad health, and it was apparent that neither were outdoors people. I remembered an old colleague of mine who ran a gardening business and after much soul searching decided to give him a ring. I suggested he visit when I wasn't there. Whether this was tactical or a cowardly ploy on my part was open for debate. He called one day, and was quickly shown around the garden, but was given the thumbs down as soon as the initial tentative price was mentioned. Meanwhile the grass was now over a foot high and the quickly spreading bushes threatened to obscure any view that he hitherto had of the garden. The problem was sorted out when I convinced Ken that another contractor who although charging the going rate, apparently did twice as much in the time as others. So in effect it was like paying someone £10 per hour. This seemed to do the trick and I left him somewhat contented but probably somewhat confused as well.

BARRiNGTON

Barrington lived in one of the southernmost towns of the county. Again not my new area normally, but he was a new referral and the support worker who usually covered that area had been laid off for the foreseeable future. Barry, as he liked to be known, lived with a development disorder, whereby he wasn't able to organise himself, everything became chaotic. He was quite happy in a flat above a bank, but the owner wanted to sell up and this included his and the flat attached. The local housing association had referred him to us as they could foresee the problem we were going to have. It was another scenario whereby a person had to downsize in theory, but still wanted all of his goods in a much-reduced area.

The flat he was to move into was one of the first the housing people had managed, seemingly many moons ago, but social housing flats were in short supply and he was grateful to have a roof over his head. He seemed quite philosophical about matters, but I suspect he wasn't aware of the three square yards of furniture to the one square yard of floor theory. Also he liked to talk and when he became fixated on a subject it was hard to get him to focus on other things. His favourite subject was local and not-so-local celebrities. He would say things like, "You'll never guess what was said to me last week, when I bumped into two members of the Pretenders?" Twenty minutes later he moved on to other unexpected meetings with his pop idols. I frequently had to bring him back from pop culture land. For instance he promised to get quotes for moving to his new flat but hadn't. The van man I'd used for moving others pleaded too busy to help. Whether he had been put off by the people I'd asked him to move in the past, I was never sure, but a substitute van man was found and we agreed a date.

When I saw Barry on the day of the move I didn't exactly notice his goods overflowing from the boxes I had obtained for him. In fact apart from covering the bottoms of the boxes, very little else had been done. It was a good job I had arrived early and I managed with limited help to get the majority of things secured one way or another. I suppose I was grateful for the limited help I had, but to be fair Barry did provide a sort of entertainment as he strutted around the floor, playing his version of 'Twist And Shout' on air guitar. When the van man arrived he threw a bit of a wobbly as he reckoned he hadn't been told about the various electrical items that seemed to have come, literally, out of the woodwork. To calm matters down I promised to help as Barry had to be out the following day at the latest. The three of us had to walk down a curving outside staircase to reach the van, which was precariously parked on the corner of a narrow street.

Because of Barry's OCD he would lock the back of the van every time he loaded boxes into it. The driver wasn't too pleased with this as he had to put the load he was carrying down to unlock it. We came to a slight compromise and removed the key from the lock but Barry would then close the door so we were still not able to access the van without putting down whatever we were carrying. Barry was better after this, following a whispered piece of advice in his ear from the van driver. It took two van-loads to clear the goods. I didn't have time to help once the job was done, but when I did call next, at his new premises he had all the stuff piled up in the bedroom and was sleeping in the lounge. I was still able to support him for a while as he made the odd appearance in the gaps between the piled-up furniture. To all intents and purposes he seemed trapped in his bedroom. Also his air guitar displays were sadly curtailed. I wasn't sure if his OCD had worsened if that was possible, but in this smaller apartment as soon as I was in through the door, he would lock it and pocket the key. He hadn't done this in the previous flat, not that I noticed anyway, but that was another item to put on the risk assessment. I was able to sort out all that was necessary in the way of paperwork following the move. The three-year contract that Festivity Support Housing had was coming to an end and there was a rumour that it wasn't worth considering its renewal.

If reports were true the total funding was at an all-time low and certainly not enough to cover twelve workers for their wages and travel expenses. In the end the rumours weren't far off the mark and Festivity Support declined to tender. The contract went back to another organisation in the county it was meant to cover, but in a vastly reduced way.

It was suggested that the reason the funding had been reduced was because some money had been diverted into giving a number of vulnerable people a monetary package for leisure and other activities. These were named direct payments, although the overall money in the system was still a fraction of what it once had been. It was particularly poignant, in that many people who previously had support from organisations that were now sadly depleted, including those that had been partly institutionalised in homes but encouraged into the community under the Supporting People umbrella, were now in danger of struggling due to cut backs. I did have the option of working for my current employer in their sheltered housing scheme as a warden. It was well run and had a good reputation but this wasn't really what I wanted to do, and so I elected for redundancy for the third time in my life. It was a particularly sad day when we all met up for one last time at the complex where we used to hold our monthly meetings. It did brighten up considerably following a pub visit with our two managers. I still see some of my colleagues now and again when we have the occasional reunion.

TWENTY-FOUR

DiPLOMACY & OUT

I probably connected in one way or other with over two hundred clients in my twelve years of being a support worker and co-ordinator. I had learnt so much, especially on the tricky diplomatic side of things. Until I got to know people I was always cagey when asking personal questions but sometimes I had to probe a bit to access the situation. One client appeared downcast when telling me of her divorce a few years previously. I hesitated to mention her marriage but when I did show sympathy about her situation and tentatively mentioned her ex, she replied, "Oh you mean the serial fornicator, I couldn't wait to get rid of him." I guess she didn't have too good a marriage.

Another lady's favourite support worker was Lauren and it was never easy standing in for her. Lauren used to pre-warn her that I was the one to visit the following week. When I arrived she would say, "Oh I was expecting Lauren, is she not coming?" She would then maintain a few minutes' silence, almost going into a sulk, before accepting a visit by a lesser person. It was always worth reminding her that she didn't look her age. For whatever reason these few words seemed to do wonders in breaking the silence.

One man I supported would come up with random comments, which initially I tended to treat in a light-hearted way. I could support him under the carers' short break funding, but was never quite sure which one of the married couple was the cared for. He wasn't able to drive so I would pick him up and we would usually end up in town. One of his questions in particular had me baffled. It was, "Suppose I saw someone go into a shoe shop, take off his shoes, try on a new pair and when staff weren't looking walk off without paying." I answered as best I could, basically stating that I would consider such an act as obviously illegal but I would wonder why the perpetrator needed to take such a risk. He would reply that perhaps there was some emotional issue that the perpetrator was able to express when doing this. After a few more conversations of a similar ilk, I realised that my service user/client was probably the perpetrator. After tentatively discussing the matter without my having to admit that I suspected him, I was fairly confident on reading between the lines, and listening without judgement that he had at last managed to overcome his shoe swapping tendency. Of course it helped that I never took him to a shoe shop, not that he ever asked me to in fairness, and as our trips were now his main outlet into town we busied ourselves with other things.

It was always difficult to know what to do in circumstances such as this, but I had no proof of wrongdoing, and he may have made up these scenarios, but it did leave me wondering why his shoes always looked immaculate and why he never felt the need to polish them.

I was asked to support an elderly man who was considered slightly vulnerable and fairly easy to be taken advantage of. Two so-called female friends would follow him to the cash point machine and although in a non-threatening, subtle way, would plead poverty according to social services. I wasn't entirely sure if it was possible to plead poverty in a subtle way but this was another scenario that I hadn't encountered before. One of the stumbling blocks was the fact that he regarded virtually everyone who spoke to him as his friend. As he was a creature of habit, I was asked to meet Alfie at about the same time he would wander into town waving his debit card about. The first time I saw him with his lady friends I used the standard pretence tactic of mentioning the fact that apparently there were some people who might regard Alfie as a free meal ticket, but I couldn't provide names as

I had no idea who they were. Could they possibly report any abusers to me? True to form they agreed with me that it was disgusting and would keep an eye on matters. Alfie was glad of my company and would always like to have a natter, but reckoned he could always open up better over a pint in Wetherspoons. I was fine with this but had learnt from a previous episode and was content with a cappuccino. Before retiring he had had a number of jobs, but preferred the open air and the days he spent as a farm hand were the best days of his life. I was able to mention our concerns and although he nodded in agreement, I knew that sooner or later friendship meant more than money and so it proved when he no longer required our services. We were satisfied he knew the situation and as he said the girls would keep others from fleecing him.

One scenario I, and probably others too, struggled with was visiting very talkative clients in very warm houses. I got on well with one lady I would visit but wished I'd advised her on the cost of heating. Whether she would have turned the heating down was open for debate but I'm sure on at least one occasion she caught me out, as she raised her voice somewhat, and disturbed me in my slumbers. Another episode to slightly sour my relationship with her was when I accompanied her to a supermarket. She was on her mobile scooter and as we approached the checkout she waited till I paid with the cash she handed to me. Thinking that she could get through the gap between checkouts and trying to encourage her to be more independent, I beckoned for her to drive forward, and suggested she could hand the money over herself. Unfortunately she misjudged the gap, hit one of the checkout stands and in a panic opened up the throttle. The scooter reared up, reminding me of a *Top Gear* stunt. It seemed to hang motionless in the air for several seconds as I grabbed her back in an endeavour to prevent her from falling backwards. Out of the corner of my eye I sensed one or two open-mouthed customers who were taking an interest in our proceedings. After a time that seemed longer than it actually was, she realised the error of her ways and the scooter resumed its rightful stance on the supermarket floor. Not long after we went back to her home in silence, she in front on her scooter, me like a naughty schoolboy following two yards behind. I wasn't invited in on this occasion.

Where I found it particularly taxing was when another person, be it a relative or a friend has to have their say, sometimes shutting out the client altogether. They wanted their interpretation on the matter, but didn't want to do anything about it themselves.

It was always difficult when speaking to professionals on behalf of a client as I had to sound as though I was on their side even if I realised it was hopeless. I may have got a reputation when I strongly argued that I thought a lady client should be on the ESA scheme and not the JSA, which she was now on. This would mean she didn't have to attend work-related seminars on a regular basis, but I knew I was up against it especially when it became apparent that I wasn't really too much of an expert on the matter.

I did quite enjoy accompanying clients to job centres. When they signed onto the jobseekers' scheme they had to indicate which job they were interested in, and a list of standard acceptable jobs was provided. They also had to select a back-up job that was not necessarily on the main list. Their choice could sometimes be interpreted as a sign that they were not too serious about looking for employment, as with one such choice that was put forward. I doubt very much that there were too many vacancies for demonstrators at The local sex shop.

A great source of help in the district were two main charities who were always good for financial support to people in difficulties. These charities had funds that we could tap into and were a godsend at times. We managed to convince social services that a lady who had applied to take back her young daughter was now in a better position, and had started to cook again thanks to funding we received for a new cooker. This was seen to be another beginning for her, and a happy outcome was achieved. Another client looking for work became more mobile thanks to the bicycle we got for him. Domestic aids that would enhance people's lives were bought, as were refurbished computers. One success saw a visually impaired lady manage to write memories of her life down with the aid of a computer programme that talked back the words and sentences she had typed in. The funding for this came from one of the charities for the blind and her remarkable story was something for her children to cherish.

Care homes held bitter-sweet emotions for me. Of all of the homes I visited I couldn't fault the care aspect. The staff I spoke to were friendly and kind enough, but I always put myself in my client's place. Would I like to end my life in one? I often surmised. Perhaps not, was the answer. I tried to adopt a positive mental attitude and saw people as carefree, spirited individuals reflecting on some happy memories. I hoped that when they left this life behind at some point, they would end up in a better world altogether. Were we, I wondered, just down here to experience the ups and downs in life, and learn from our mistakes as best we could? This in turn would hopefully stand us in good stead for what was to come, and did the Buddhists know something I didn't? Was it possible that we had many lives and during each one our souls became more advanced until such time as we learnt all that was expected of us? If that was the case and in relating to a well-known board game I felt I'd climbed at least two rungs of the spiritual ladder, either that or I had slipped several squares down the descending snake.

When I was a lot younger I mistakenly assumed that the vast majority of people once they retired automatically reduced their workload accordingly. This was not borne out in my observation of some of my clients. Those who had been busy for most of their life often found it difficult to let go although it did help if they possessed an artistic bent or other creative attributes. My father-in-law for instance was very skilled at making anything in metal and had planned his retirement down to a fine degree. He had built an eighteen-foot-long shed to house all manner of engineering tools, as well as two lathes, various drills and a very heavy cast iron milling machine. I actually gave a hand when we tried to manoeuvre it. Three of us snaked it through a narrow passageway between two Victorian terraced houses, on a wheelbarrow. In hindsight it wasn't exactly the best vehicle for transporting a sixty-year old monstrosity. By the time we finished with it, it was incapable of carrying the weight of any more heavy industrial machines, or anything else for that matter.

When I left clients for the last time I made a point of never asking how they were getting on at a later date. At least I could always imagine them as still alive and kicking, not yet ready to exit the departure lounge. I did make an exception on a couple of occasions and one in particular had me wishing that I'd left my identity badge behind. The client, an elderly man in his eighties, was asleep in the lounge of the care home. I sat down beside him and gently whispered his name. The lady resident who sat next to him eyed me in horror. "Can't you see he's asleep?" she shouted. "And besides we don't want any more doctors in here, thank you, we've got enough of our own." By now other residents in the lounge were looking at me as though I was a pariah. I wasn't quite sure which way to turn.

"I'm his support worker," I countered in a voice I hoped the others wouldn't hear, "and not a doctor."

"Speak up Doctor," she shouted. I just hoped I wouldn't get a queue of residents lining up ready to tell me about their ailments. Again I repeated my status as a support worker, but she persisted. "Please go now, I told you we don't need the likes of you round here." I ignored this piece of so-called advice despite her hostile glare. I felt compelled to wait a while longer but realised Ralph wasn't going to wake any time soon. "Are you still here?" came the latest verbal onslaught. I decided to leave and ring later to see how he was faring. As I left there was one more parting comment. "Don't come back, thank you." I didn't mind scenarios like this; it meant at least some of the residents hadn't lost their spirit.

In 2015 I attended an appointment at the job centre. It seemed odd to be in there for myself but I went ahead and signed on the dole; two days later I changed my mind and became one of life's early retirees and could be seen around the usual haunts, B&Q and the like. I now had to contemplate life's older people's problems. Should I have been upset that I hadn't been given senior rates on my entry into a leisure park with the family or was it a form of compliment that they thought I was younger than I was? I was now into the realms of serious retirement conundrums.

I wasn't sure if buying a book entitled *1001 Paintings to See Before You Die* was a good idea, but I trust that the powers that be, extend my life expectancy because of it, as in two years I've only seen seven of them.

A married couple who were friends of mine had not long moved to Abergavenny and as I was into hill climbing, a gang of us would take it in turns to drive to the Black Mountains or the Brecon Beacons, and meet one or both at a pre-selected spot. These jaunts would occupy a good chunk of the day, usually on a weekend and I could always rely on a good night's sleep because of the day's activities. I was open to most activity-based pursuits, lest I slipped into becoming a pipe and slippers man.

There were moments in 2003 when I almost changed my mind about applying for redundancy. I was in a secure engineering job and although from time to time we experienced a few redundancies, usually every four years, seemingly just after the start of the Olympics, I never thought I was in any danger. If I was serious about it I would have to really push. Two of my children had left home but there were still two others who remained and relied on me for the usual financial upkeeps. Although my wages weren't jaw dropping they were adequate and with my understanding wife's wages, we lived a comfortable existence. It also helped that I worked overtime. Besides a few hours during the average working week I was to be seen at my engineering job most Saturday mornings, which although very inconvenient to my social and family life, we accepted it as an everyday part of working life. I suppose I went on the general assumption that one could never get enough. Most families will testify that any spare money that they think they have, soon seems to disappear.

Towards the end of my engineering career I found myself clock-watching and becoming increasingly bored with mundane tasks, and my determination to get out won through. I had applied for a job in the previous October with a well-known charity supporting those with conditions such as cerebral palsy but wasn't successful in securing the post. I was however offered a post as a bank staff member, which after suitable training I might be called upon to put in a shift, as and when. I accepted this position, cut back on overtime and worked the occasional duty with the charity under the guise of relief working. This in itself gave me the courage to put in for redundancy knowing that at least I had some work to fall back on. As it happened I was able to secure permanent jobs within weeks of leaving engineering and also said goodbye to bank working.

Looking back on my working life I suppose I hadn't had to take a massive gamble in changing vocations. I had been in a rut and was not one to take too many chances in life. But talking to others who seemed to experience similar conundrums and looked elsewhere, I was assured that despite a drop in their finances they found that to their surprise they were more than able to cope. I also experienced this fact and was duly surprised myself. Was there some sort of metaphysical law at work here that compensated a person who was determined to change their working life in order to support those less fortunate? Another plus besides having job satisfaction was meeting a whole array of people from all walks of life, many of them characters in their own right. During my last twelve years of working I learnt so much about life, about myself, about humanity in general, and was quite content to be one of life's "also-rans". All we can do morally and humanly speaking is to leave this world with more credits than debits to our name, although in my case I just hope it's not exactly a close-run thing.

AUTHOR BIO:

Graham Phipps lives in Herefordshire and is married with four children and and numerous grandchildren. He started writing articles for various magazines in his forties as a hobby, but on experiencing some humorous often complex situations with his new job, he felt compelled to share his experiences.

 Matador

For exclusive discounts on Matador titles,
sign up to our occasional newsletter at
troubador.co.uk/bookshop